Nostromo

Cedric Watts is Professor of English at the University of Sussex. He is the author of the following works: *Conrad's 'Heart of Darkness': A Critical and Contextual Discussion*, 1977; *Cunninghame Graham: A Critical Biography* (co-author: Laurence Davies), 1979; *A Preface to Conrad*, 1982; *R. B. Cunninghame Graham*, 1983; *The Deceptive Text: An Introduction to Covert Plots*, 1984; *A Preface to Keats,*1985; *William Shakespeare: 'Measure for Measure'*, 1986; *Hamlet*, 1988; *Joseph Conrad: A Literary Life*, 1989. He has edited various books, including: *Joseph Conrad's Letters to R. B. Cunninghame Graham*, 1969; *The English Novel*, 1976; *Selected Writings of Cunninghame Graham*, 1981; and the following works of Joseph Conrad: *Lord Jim* (co-editor: Robert Hampson), 1986; *'Typhoon' and Other Tales*, 1986; *The Nigger of the 'Narcissus'*, 1988; and *'Heart of Darkness' and Other Tales*, 1990.

Penguin Critical Studies
Advisory Editors
Stephen Coote and Bryan Loughrey

Joseph Conrad

Nostromo

Cedric Watts

Penguin Books

PENGUIN BOOKS

Published by the Penguin Group
27 Wrights Lane, London, W8 5TZ, England
Viking Penguin Inc., 40 West 23rd Street, New York, New York 10010, USA
Penguin Books Australia Ltd, Ringwood, Victoria, Australia
Penguin Books Canada Ltd, 2801 John Street, Markham, Ontario, Canada, L3R 1B4
Penguin Books (NZ) Ltd, 182–190 Wairau Road, Auckland 10, New Zealand

Penguin Books Ltd, Registered Offices: Harmondsworth, Middlesex, England

First published 1990

Made and printed in Great Britain by
Richard Clay Ltd, Bungay, Suffolk
Filmset in 9 pt Monophoto Times

To LINDA WATTS *(1964–1985)*

Contents

Part 1 Preliminary Matter

1.1 Acknowledgements and Editorial Notes

When preparing this book, I was particularly indebted to the following works. Jocelyn Baines: *Joseph Conrad: A Critical Biography* (London: Weidenfeld & Nicolson, 1960); Norman Sherry: *Conrad's Western World* (London: Cambridge University Press, 1971); Zdzisław Najder: *Joseph Conrad: A Chronicle* (Cambridge: Cambridge University Press, 1983); *The Collected Letters of Joseph Conrad*, edited by Frederick R. Karl and Laurence Davies (Cambridge: Cambridge University Press, 1983 on); and Yves Hervouet: 'Conrad and Anatole France' in *Ariel* I (1970), pp. 84–99. I am grateful to the Longman Group Ltd for permission to adapt some material which originally appeared in my *Preface to Conrad* (London and New York: Longman, 1982). Ian Watt's *Joseph Conrad: 'Nostromo'* (Cambridge: Cambridge University Press, 1988) helpfully suggested ways in which I might revise and augment my previous arguments. Brian Nicholas aided the French translations; Hans van Marle provided shrewd advice, as usual; and Dr Geoffrey Hemstedt kindly helped to check the proofs.

Unless otherwise indicated, all quotations from the book of *Nostromo* are from the first British trade edition (London: Harper & Brothers, 1904). I have selected this edition because of its literary-historical importance: Conrad anxiously studied the reviews it received; and therefore the present reader should see the text that those early reviewers read, rather than the variant text of one of the subsequent editions. Furthermore, that Harper volume contains some important material which does not appear in current, commonly used texts of *Nostromo*. Conrad's accentuation of Spanish names was often erratic or incorrect; I have preserved his accentuation when quoting the novel, but have endeavoured to supply correct accentuation in my commentary.

In any quotation, a row of three points (...) indicates an ellipsis already present in the printed text, whereas a row of five points indicates an omission that I have made. To comply with Penguin's 'house style', outer quotation-marks are single and not double. All other emendations to quoted passages (occasional clarifications, or grammatical adaptations of quotations to their context of commentary) are given within

1

square brackets. With these exceptions, I have endeavoured to present all quoted material without correction or alteration.

This book was written in 1988.

1.2 The Plan of This Book

This book is concerned with the genesis, meaning and value of Conrad's greatest long novel, *Nostromo*. I assume that some of my readers will be novices who know little of Conrad and his range, that others will have some familiarity with the area, and that others will be specialists. I've attempted to include something for everybody. Part 2 offers a brief survey of Conrad's life, bearing in mind that the originality of *Nostromo* is largely a consequence of the author's strikingly distinctive career as a Polish-born seaman who eventually became a British fiction-writer. Part 3 discusses the cultural and historical background to the novel, and gives samples of source-material. Part 4 scans in diverse ways the contents of *Nostromo*, paying particular attention to the meanings of its techniques; and Part 5 appraises a selection of critical approaches. Thus, instead of providing a commentary which closely follows the consecutive chapters of the novel, I have adopted a more flexible approach which, by indicating a diversity of perspectives, may imply sympathy with *Nostromo*'s mobility of viewpoint.

Obviously, my apparent distinction between 'contexts' and 'contents' (Parts 3 and 4) is merely a tactic of presentation. The novel's sources may be part of its context, but their adaptation by Conrad forms part of the content. Similarly, a critical analysis may be predominantly concerned with the novel's content, but it will nevertheless incorporate assumptions about the historical and cultural background of the work. A monograph imposes a linear, consecutive sequence on responses which present themselves to the mind less as sequences than as mobile, interlinked and interchanging clusters. Finally, I am delighted to concede what critics sometimes conceal: namely, that Conrad's articulate intelligence and articulate sensibility are so powerful that the rich eloquence of *Nostromo* mocks the greyly rational prose of most commentaries. My book proffers aids to the comprehension of *Nostromo*; the more the aids succeed, the sooner they may be discarded.

Part 2 Biographical

2.1 Thematic Introduction

Janus is the two-faced god: he looks in opposite directions at the same time. Hence the term 'janiform': a janiform person is radically paradoxical in outlook; and a janiform literary text is one which is centrally or importantly paradoxical or even self-contradictory. Joseph Conrad is such a person, and *Nostromo* is such a text. Conrad once remarked, 'Homo duplex has in my case more than one meaning.'[1] *Homo duplex*: the double man. Conrad was Polish and English; seaman and writer; Catholic and atheist; moralist and sceptic; Augustan and Romantic; rationalist and anti-rationalist; conservative and subversive.

In 'A Familiar Preface', he affirmed his commitment to 'a few very simple ideas', notably 'the idea of Fidelity'; but the same essay declares of the artist:

In that interior world where his thought and his emotions go seeking for the experience of imagined adventures, there are no policemen, no law, no pressure of circumstance or dread of opinion to keep him within bounds.[2]

He said that 'The sight of human affairs deserves admiration and pity'; yet, though he denounced anarchism as 'a brazen cheat', he could remark:

Society is fundamentally criminal – or it would not exist. Selfishness preserves everything . . . . . That is why I respect the extreme anarchists. – 'I hope for general extermination'. Very well. It's justifiable and, moreover, it is plain.[3]

Having declared that 'There is no morality, no knowledge and no hope', he said that the first requirement of an artist should be 'the cherishing of an undying hope'; and the claim that 'The fate of a humanity condemned ultimately to perish from cold is not worth troubling about' came from the man who was to say: 'What one feels so hopelessly barren in declared pessimism is just its arrogance.'[4]

Conrad's personality can sometimes appear a turbulent battleground of conflicting ideas, beliefs, attitudes and arguments; but that turbulence generated a sequence of literary works which includes some of the finest tales and novels in the language. His art, at its best, aspires to the condition of paradox: it has its traditional and popular elements, yet also a radicalism of conception which enables it to anticipate the developments which were to become known as Modernism and Deconstructionism.[5] He commends traditional values: heroism, honesty, fidelity, kindness; yet he subjects them to the tests of a corrosive scepticism. In turn, he is often Pyrrhonistic, for he is prepared to be sceptical even about scepticism itself. In richly eloquent language he offers warnings about eloquence; with long-sighted vision he portrays human myopia; he comprehends and communicates a vista of human incomprehension and failures of communication. *Nostromo* is variously wise, bleak, taxing, bewildering, searching, prophetic, comic, satiric, deeply ironic and vividly cinematic. It has some flaws. But it remains a triumph of creative energy: proof that a life fraught with tensions and contradictions can produce a text which helps to define and maintain the beleaguered values of civilization.

2.2 Conrad's Life

2.2.1 EARLY YEARS

'. . . . . [W]e had once more to murmur "*Væ Victis*" ["Woe to the Conquered"] and count the cost in sorrow. Not that we were ever very good at calculating, either, in prosperity or adversity. That's a lesson we could never learn, to the exasperation of our enemies who have bestowed on us the epithet of Incorrigible . . .'

The speaker was of Polish nationality, that nationality not so much alive as surviving, which persists in thinking, breathing, speaking, hoping, and suffering in its grave, railed in by a million of bayonets and triple-sealed with the seals of three great empires . . . . .

[P]atriotism – a somewhat discredited sentiment, because the delicacy of our humanitarians regards it as a relic of barbarism.

Conrad: 'Prince Roman'

Nostromo, which first appeared in 1904, is arguably the most brilliant of political novels. It's rich, vivid, colourful, paradoxical; from a host of particular details it generates a peculiarly persuasive account of the evolution of a new republic; and, in its comprehensive and sceptical view of economic imperialism, it seems to be intelligently of its times and prophetically ahead of them. If we seek a biographical explanation of Conrad's exceptional achievement, one factor soon emerges.

In December 1857, Joseph Conrad – then Józef Teodor Konrad Korzeniowski – was born into a Poland which had vanished from the map of Europe. In a series of 'partitions' (1772, 1793, 1795) Poland had been engorged by Russia from the east and by Prussia and Austria from the west and south-west. The infant Conrad was Polish by heritage but Russian by enforced circumstances. If Conrad could revisit Poland today, he would find wearisomely familiar the fact that Poland is part of the Russian empire; but he would also find encouragingly familiar the stubborn spirit of independence and the hunger for individual and national freedom which is still alive among many of its people. His essays 'The Crime of Partition' and 'Autocracy and War' were to celebrate that spirit and condemn sardonically the nation's oppressors – a condemnation which prior and subsequent events so fully vindicate.

Conrad's father, Apollo Korzeniowski, was a member of the land-owning gentry. He had little aptitude for practical business matters, though he worked for a time as an estate manager; his real interests were literature and Polish politics. He wrote comedies and mystically patriotic poems, and translated works by Shakespeare, Dickens, Victor Hugo and Alfred de Vigny. In 1856 he married Ewelina (Ewa) Bobrowska, a young woman of another prosperous land-owning family. Conrad was to be their only child. To commemorate his son's baptism, Apollo Korzeniowski composed a poem which is dated 'in the 85th year of Russian tyranny' and ends thus:

My child, my son – tell yourself that you are without land, without love, without Fatherland, without humanity – so long as Poland, our Mother, is enslaved.[6]

In Warsaw, Apollo became one of the leaders of the 'Reds', the more extreme of the two main patriotic parties: it advocated the liberation of the serfs as well as violent action to regain national independence. On his initiative was formed the underground committee which was eventually to launch the bloodily suppressed insurrection of 1863. But in 1861 Apollo himself was arrested and imprisoned; both he and Ewa were sentenced to exile for their subversive activities, and their four-year-old son accompanied them on the bitter journey to the remote Russian province of Vologda. This period of exile sapped Ewa's health: after her return, ailing with advanced tuberculosis, she died in 1865 at the age of thirty-two. Consequently, Apollo became a brooding, melancholy figure, possessed by a rather morbid religiosity. He wrote:

I have kept my eyes fixed on the Cross and by that means fortified my fainting soul and reeling brain. The sacred days of agony have passed, and I resume my ordinary life, a little more broken but with breath still in me, still alive. But the little orphan is always at my side, and I never forget my anxiety for him . . . . . [H]e grows up as though in a monastic cell. For the *memento mori* we have the grave of our dear one . . . . .[7]

On 23 May 1869 Apollo, in turn, died of tuberculosis, and Conrad was thus an eleven-year-old orphan. He followed his father's coffin in a funeral procession through the streets of Kraków: a procession which, as he later recalled, was also a huge national demonstration:

What I saw with my own eyes was the public funeral, the cleared streets, the hushed crowds; but I understood perfectly well that this was a manifestation of the national spirit seizing a worthy occasion. That bareheaded mass of work people, youths of the University, women at the windows, school-boys on the pavement, could have known nothing positive about him except the fame of his fidelity to the one guiding emotion in their hearts.[8]

The young Conrad had thus learnt bitterly and directly the lessons which were eventually to become implicit in the rich fabric of *Nostromo*: the price exacted in personal and familial terms by the ideals, rhetoric and illusions of politics.

Conrad's uncle, Tadeusz Bobrowski, now became his guardian. Bobrowski was wealthy, astute, and unfailingly conscientious in his guardianship, which extended until his death a quarter of a century later. He repeatedly emphasized (and exaggerated) a contrast between two sides of his ward's family. The Korzeniowski heritage, he claimed, was characterized by impractical idealism, by romantic dreams and moody waywardness; whereas the Bobrowski heritage was characterized by sober, steady diligence, and by a recognition of the need to come to terms with hard realities. Biographers have pointed out that the contrast was by no means as clear-cut as Bobrowski suggested, for 'all his brothers were hotheads' and two of them 'held political views similar to Apollo's'.[9] Nevertheless, what was repeatedly impressed upon Conrad was the sense of a paradoxical inheritance: the quixotic versus the practical, the visionary versus the sceptically pragmatic. In his eventual novels, those contending forces provided the dynamics.

Conrad's schooling appears to have been irregular and unsystematic (he claimed to have enjoyed geography most), but Bobrowski provided a private tutor, Adam Pulman. Neither the tutor nor the uncle was able to dissuade Conrad from his youthful ambition – inspired partly by novels and travel-books – of going to sea; and so, at the age of sixteen, the prospective mariner left Poland for the south of France and the port of Marseille. There Conrad enjoyed the cosmopolitan social life, mixing with fishermen and businessmen, travellers and artists, and worked both as a pilot and as a hand on sailing-ships. He voyaged to the West Indies on the *Mont-Blanc*, a three-masted wooden barque; initially he was a passenger, but on the second voyage he served as an apprentice. Then in 1876 he was enrolled as a steward on another three-master, the *Saint-Antoine*, which (he later hinted) carried arms to the conservative rebels in Colombia – and may thus have provided ideas for the eventual *Nostromo*. He subsequently claimed to have seen Puerto Cabello and La Guaira in Venezuela, to have gone ashore for a few days 'on that dreary coast' and to have 'had a distant view of Caracas'.[10] The first mate of the *Saint-Antoine* was Dominic Cervoni, broad-chested and vain – 'His thick black moustaches, curled every morning with hot tongs by the barber at the corner of the quay, seemed to hide a perpetual smile'[11] – and later to be reincarnated as Nostromo and as the Dominic of *The Arrow of Gold*. Conrad's reminiscences were to emphasize Dominic Cervoni's proud assurance, resourcefulness and ruthless capability, as well as a capacity for lawless maritime escapades. In one of those volumes of reminiscence, *The Mirror of the Sea*, Conrad says that he joined Dominic in a syndicate which smuggled arms from Marseille along the coast to Spanish Carlists, the royalists who supported the Pretender, Don Carlos. According to Conrad, the syndicate was betrayed to the authorities by Dominic's nephew, César; their vessel, the *Tremolino*, was pursued by coastguards; the crew wrecked her to escape the pursuers, and during the crisis Dominic hurled his nephew (who happened to be weighted with stolen gold) to death in the foaming sea. There is no doubt that Conrad's reminiscences, while purportedly factual, have been infiltrated by fictional devices: Norman Sherry's researches have shown that though Dominic was known to be a smuggler, César was not killed at sea but lived on to marry and have a son; he died at a ripe age in 1926 – thus having outlived by two years the author who had depicted his watery demise.[12]

The young Conrad was adventurous, sensitive, temperamental and sometimes depressive. His long-suffering Uncle Tadeusz, who regularly supplied his errant nephew with funds, wrote to a Polish friend:

I was absolutely certain that he was already somewhere in the Antipodes, when suddenly, amidst all the business at the Kiev Fair in 1878, I received a telegram: 'Conrad blessé envoyez argent – arrivez' ['Conrad wounded send money – come'].[13]

Conrad's troubles had begun when he found that as an alien he was barred by law from French ships; nor did he have a consular permit for service at the port.

While still in possession of the 3,000 fr[ancs] sent to him for the voyage, he met his former Captain, Mr. Duteil, who persuaded him to participate in some enterprise on the coasts of Spain – some kind of contraband! He invested 1,000 fr[ancs] in it and made over 400 which pleased them greatly so that on the second occasion he put in all he had – and lost the lot.

Heavily in debt, Conrad borrowed a further 800 francs from a friend, went to Villefranche to try to join an American squadron; failed; and finally in desperation gambled away the 800 francs at Monte Carlo.

Having managed his affairs so excellently he returns to Marseilles and one fine evening invites his friend the creditor to tea, and before his arrival attempts to take his life with a revolver. (Let this detail remain between us, as I have been telling everyone that he was wounded in a duel . . . . .) The bullet goes durch und durch [through and through] near his heart without damaging any vital organ.

Bobrowski paid the debts, 'influenced by considerations of our national honour' as well as by family loyalty, while Conrad recovered from the deep wound in the chest.

My study of the Individual has convinced me that he is not a bad boy, only one who is extremely sensitive, conceited, reserved, and in addition excitable. In short I found in him all the defects of the Nałęcz family. He is able and eloquent . . . . . very popular with his captains and also with the sailors . . . . . In his ideas and discussions he is ardent and original . . . . . and is an imperialist. De gustibus non est disputandum [There's no point in disputing about tastes] . . . . .

Finally, it was agreed that Conrad should join the British Merchant Navy ('where there are no such formalities as in France'), and four years after leaving Poland he arrived at Lowestoft on the coal freighter *Mavis*.

2.2.2 MARITIME YEARS

Conrad's beginnings in England could scarcely have been humbler. He obtained a berth on a small coaster, the barquentine *Skimmer of the Sea*, which carried coals down the east coast from Newcastle to Lowestoft; and his wage was a mere one shilling per month, when even the ship's boy received twenty-five shillings. Two and a half years later, she sank at sea, drowning some of his former shipmates; but by then he had graduated to larger vessels on longer voyages. He worked for a while on the wool-clipper *Duke of Sutherland*, which plied between London and Sydney; and steadily, over the subsequent sixteen years, with numerous voyages on ships ranging from elegant three-masters to rusty tramp-steamers, he rose in rank: third mate, second mate, skipper. Repeatedly on the great ocean-going sailing-ships he made the run between England, Bombay and Australia; gradually, struggling with the wayward English language, he learned the rules of seamanship and passed the successive inquisitorial examinations; and, at last, in 1886, at the age of twenty-eight, he not only gained his master's certificate but also acquired British nationality. Tadeusz Bobrowski was delighted by the double achievement: he had long urged his nephew to relinquish Russian citizenship and become 'a free citizen of a free country'.[14] Ford Madox Hueffer, subsequently Conrad's literary collaborator, was to recall Britain's reputation in Europe as a land of liberty: the 'England of Conrad's early vision', he declared, was 'an immense power standing for liberty and hospitality for refugees; vigilant over a pax Britannica that embraced the world'.[15]

Culturally, Conrad's upbringing had been anglophile. As recently as the 1850s, the British at Crimea had fought the Poles' most hated oppressors, the Russians; and Conrad would, as writer, eventually offer warm tributes to that 'liberty, which can only be found under the English flag'.[16] It was in the service of the 'pax Britannica that embraced the world' that Conrad repeatedly voyaged the globe, whether to Bombay, Singapore or Melbourne. This was the last great era of sail, of the full-rigged iron sailing-ships like the *Tilkhurst*, which carried jute from Calcutta to Dundee (Conrad was her second mate in 1886; she endured until 1923), or of majestic clippers like the *Torrens*, famed for speed and beauty, which carried wool from Adelaide to London during the years when Conrad was her first mate. In the late nineteenth century, over half the shipping of the world belonged to the British Merchant Navy; and, as Zdzisław Najder points out, 'since sailors were in considerable demand, no special permits were required for the enlistment of foreigners'.[17] The young Pole who had once declared himself 'an imperialist' was now serving an empire which, between 1875 and 1900, added nearly 5 million square miles to its extent, to make a total of some 13 million square miles with 320 million people.

Conrad's motivation in going to sea had, in part, been literary and romantic. The essay 'Geography and Some Explorers' (published in 1924, at the end of his life) vividly conveys those days of childhood when his imagination had been fired by the reading of books of travel and exploration, like McClintock's *The Voyage of the 'Fox'*, the story of Mungo Park, or the adventures of Bruce in Abyssinia: his tutor had said that he seemed to have been wasting his time in reading books of travel instead of attending to his studies.[18] Certainly Conrad was to gain experience of some of the remotest and least civilized parts of the globe –

Java, Sumatra, Borneo; and certainly he felt the excitements and the pleasures of oceanic voyages under sail. But he also learnt the harsh realities of dangerous toil. At that time, deaths at sea by shipwreck were a common occurrence; of the first seven British ships on which he sailed, no fewer than five were lost during a four-year period; and the *Palestine* voyage was to provide him with an unforgettable initiation into peril. The *Palestine*, an old and decrepit barque, left Newcastle for Bangkok with a cargo of coal; but after three hundred miles she lost her sails in a gale, sprang a leak, and returned to England for repairs, which took eight months. At the second attempt the vessel voyaged from September to March, reaching the Bangka Strait off Sumatra, before disaster struck. In the words of the Court of Inquiry:

[S]moke was discovered issuing from the coals . . . . . Water was thrown over them until the smoke abated, the boats were lowered, water placed in them. On the 13th some coals were thrown overboard, about 4 tons, and more water poured down the hold. On the 14th, the hatches being on but not battened down, the decks blew up fore and aft as far as the poop . . . . . [A]bout 11 p.m. the vessel was a mass of fire . . . . .[19]

The ship sank, and Conrad reached shore in a lifeboat; an experience to be recalled more than fifteen years later in the tale 'Youth'. Indeed, so many of his maritime experiences were eventually to be recalled in his reminiscences and works of fiction that his motives in going to sea may appear to have been *doubly* literary: not only had his imagination been fired by his reading of adventurous explorations, but also he must have sensed that his own odysseys through the world could provide the basis of a second career, as a writer. Another reason for that transition was certainly his increasing recognition of contradictions between romantic hopes and harsh realities, and between the rhetoric of imperialism and its sordid manifestations. Again, 'Geography and Some Explorers' graphically makes this point. Conrad recalled that at school he had once put his finger on a white spot in the middle of the map of Africa, and had boasted that one day he would go there. In 1890, during his service with a company responsible for exploiting the Belgian Congo, he found himself on a stern-wheel steamboat at Stanley Falls.

I said to myself with awe, 'This is the very spot of my boyish boast.'
    A great melancholy descended on me. Yes, this was the very spot. But there was no shadowy friend to stand by my side in the night of the enormous wilderness, no great haunting memory, but only the unholy recollection of a prosaic newspaper 'stunt' and the distasteful knowledge of the vilest scramble for

loot that ever disfigured the history of human conscience and geographical exploration. What an end to the idealized realities of a boy's daydreams![20]

The 'vilest scramble for loot' was one of the most predatory aspects of the competition between the great European powers to seize parts of Africa: the ruthless system of King Leopold II of Belgium for extorting rubber and ivory from the Congo. The hapless Congolese inhabitants were subjected to conscription, coercion, mutilations and summary executions. Conrad observed, made his notes, reflected, and eventually, in 1899, was to publish 'Heart of Darkness', his most brilliant tale; a novella unparalleled in the satiric scorn of its indictment of imperialism. Already, on that perilous African journey, Conrad carried with him the unfinished manuscript of his first novel, *Almayer's Folly*. In 1895 that book was published by T. Fisher Unwin of London, who paid the author just £20 for it; and Conrad's literary career was thus publicly inaugurated.

2.2.3 LITERARY CAREER

There was no clean break between the maritime career and the literary career: during his early struggles to pay his way as a writer, Conrad would often keep in mind the possibility of returning to sea; and, as late as 1898, he visited ship-owners in Glasgow in the hope of securing another command. He was, however, obliged to come to terms with the evolution of the Merchant Navy. As ocean-crossing ships became larger and more efficient, there were fewer opportunities for qualified mates and captains to gain employment. Between 1875 and 1894 the total tonnage of British shipping had risen from 6,153,000 to 8,956,000; but in the same period the number of vessels registered with the British Merchant Navy had diminished from 25,461 to 21,206; and, of the sailing ships in this number, there had been a steep decline from 21,291 to 12,943 – so that Conrad, whose experience was predominantly with sail, stood at a disadvantage. On average, 260 masters were becoming unemployed each year.[21]

In the world of literary publications, on the other hand, circumstances were exceptionally propitious. First, during the nineteenth century a variety of technological advances had reduced the costs of paper, printing and book-production. Secondly, as the electorate of a soaring British population was increased by the Reform Bills of 1832 and particularly of 1867, governments saw the merits of 'civilizing' the electorate by educational reform. The Education Act of 1870, for example, established locally elected school boards which could compel attendance to the age of thirteen (fees being waived for poorer parents), and a huge school-building programme proceeded. Handsome public libraries were erected in towns and cities, while commercial subscription-libraries could dispatch books to subscribers in the remoter regions. It was estimated that whereas in 1841, 67 per cent of males and 51 per cent of females were literate, by 1900 the figures had risen to 97 per cent and 96 per cent respectively. Publishing houses multiplied to meet the needs of an expanding readership; a diversity of magazines flourished. At the census of 1861, 3,400 respondents identified themselves as authors, editors or journalists; by 1891, the figure was 6,000; by 1901, 11,000.[22]

Conrad chose to write in English rather than in Polish or French; and that choice gave him potential access to a vast international English-speaking readership. Particularly fortunate for someone embarking on a literary career in the 1890s was the fact that international agreements to regulate copyright had at last been established: especially important for Conrad's prospects was the Chace Act of 1891, whereby the United States of America agreed to respect the copyright of British authors. What enabled Conrad to survive as a writer was the fact that it was now possible for an author to be paid numerous times for the same piece of work. A novel might first be serialized in a magazine in Great Britain, then in a magazine in the United States; next it would appear as a book not only in Britain but also, virtually simultaneously, in the USA. (Magazines often provided generous payment: between 1865 and 1905, Henry James's income from the serialization of his works greatly exceeded that from his books.) Then there might be 'colonial' editions for Australia or Canada, and European versions in English or in translation. Indeed, when we look back at the diversity of markets for literary material of all kinds – but particularly for novels, tales and essays – the 1890s resemble a Golden Age for the aspiring writer.

Conrad also knew that there was a continuing appetite for tales of travel, of voyages and of exotic locations: Rider Haggard's novels had annexed Africa; Kipling was making wealth from his Indian experiences; Robert Louis Stevenson's fiction roamed the world. In *Almayer's Folly*, Conrad laid literary claim to the Malay Archipelago, making his début with a sombrely atmospheric narrative of intrigue and disillusionment among striving individuals who seemed to be mocked by the fecund vastness of the tropical jungle and the serene indifference of the ocean. This novel was in some ways cumbrous and laboured, but it was sardonic in its ironies and potent in its rich thematic and descriptive textures. (The plotting was so subtle that its covert plot was not identified until nearly ninety years later.)[23] On its appearance, *Almayer's Folly* was well publicized and very widely reviewed, though the reviews were mixed. A few critics were sneering or derisory ('Borneo is a fine field for the study of monkeys, not of men'); most spoke with respect modulating to enthusiasm; and some hailed the arrival of a writer of genius. A large number of reviewers emphasized the work's originality and power. Conrad was frequently compared with Kipling; and even when the reviewer concluded that he was Kipling's inferior, the comparison was still flattering, given that in the mid-1890s many British reviewers regarded Kipling as the leading contemporary writer. The *Spectator* prophesied that 'Joseph Conrad . . . . . might become the Kipling of the Malay Archipelago', while the *Manchester Guardian* later claimed that he was 'as masculine as Kipling, but without that parade of masculinity which Kipling loves'.[24]

Conrad, who studied the reviews closely and anxiously, had good reason to feel proud of his achievement. After twenty arduous years at sea he had gained a foothold as a writer in an alien and difficult language: 'I had to work like a coal miner in his pit quarrying all my English sentences out of a black night,' he recalled.[25] He was to remain a writer until his death in 1924. Had he foreseen the full anguish of his literary struggles, however, it is doubtful that he would ever have embarked on *Almayer's Folly*. He sought to maintain the life-style of a middle-class gentleman or rural squire; but repeatedly, until the eventual success of *Chance* in 1914, he had to struggle with debt, ill-health (gout, depression, breakdown), and the frustration of learning that a high literary reputation was no guarantor of commercial success. Furthermore, he soon bore the responsibilities of a father: in 1896 he married Jessie George, an industrious young typist by whom he had two sons: Borys (born in 1898) and John (1906).

Almayer's Folly was followed within a year by its sequel, *An Outcast of the Islands* (1896), which dealt with the same location and an earlier stage in the saga of Tom Lingard. Conrad then endeavoured to develop the Lingard saga into a trilogy with his third novel of the Malay Archipelago, *The Rescuer* (eventually re-titled *The Rescue*); but this work caused him such extreme creative difficulty that he took more than twenty years to complete it. There was another false start with *The Sisters*, the story of a sensitive young artist, a Slav who comes to live in Paris; only a fragment survived, to be published posthumously. And in 1896–7 he published in magazines the remarkably uneven quartet of tales

('Karain', 'The Lagoon', 'The Idiots' and 'An Outpost of Progress')
which, with the 'left-handed production' entitled 'The Return', were to
comprise the volume *Tales of Unrest*. In this phase he was clearly
experimenting with different locations, modes and styles; the results
were erratic in quality, but they preserved a thematic identity. All
display an imaginative preoccupation with human isolation in a harsh
cosmos, with illusions and disillusionment, with failures of communication and with the mocking silence of death. Already he was anticipating
Nostromo by his interest in obsessed treasure-seekers (Lingard, Almayer),
in the beguiled or disillusioned colonialist, and in the treachery entailed
by the pursuit of wealth.

In 1897 began his major phase as a writer, which extended until 1911.
Works of this phase include *The Nigger of the 'Narcissus'*, 'Youth',
'Heart of Darkness', *Lord Jim*, 'Typhoon', *Nostromo*, *The Secret Agent*,
'The Secret Sharer', *Under Western Eyes* and 'A Smile of Fortune'. This
is a period of astonishing richness, variety and mastery, displaying
exuberant descriptive vividness, thematic and symbolic sophistication,
and a keen philosophical and political scepticism. Some of the reviewers
were obtuse or grudging, but on the whole Conrad received ample and
gratifying recognition. In particular, Edward Garnett, the leading 'literary midwife' of the day (who worked successively as publisher's reader
for Fisher Unwin, Heinemann, Duckworth and other firms) seized every
opportunity in the review-columns to proclaim Conrad's brilliance.
Conrad's fame spread widely, aided largely by the initial publication of
his works in magazines and journals at home and abroad. This was also
the period in which he came into personal contact with some of the
leading writers of the day. R. B. Cunninghame Graham, the aristocratic
socialist and adventurer, became a close friend; Ford Madox Hueffer
became a valued collaborator; John Galsworthy maintained a fraternal
correspondence and provided loans; Stephen Crane, the short-lived
American author, entered a brief, touching friendship; Kipling sent a
flattering letter; and other contacts were with Henry James, H. G. Wells
and George Bernard Shaw. The south-to-south-east corner of England
seems to have been well populated with writers: Kipling at Rottingdean
(later Burwash) in Sussex; Hueffer, Crane, Garnett and subsequently
Conrad himself at Pent Farm, near Hythe in Kent; James at Rye, Wells
at Sandgate; and all, thanks to the excellent railway services, were within
easy commuting distance of London.

Although Conrad's fame grew steadily, this did not make his task of
writing any easier. Creative work imposed such intense nervous strain

upon him that the completion of a novel was sometimes followed by a virtual breakdown: his wife reported that on finishing *Under Western Eyes* he lay in bed 'mixed up in the scenes and hold[ing] converse with the characters'.[26] Yet after such deranging struggles, the material rewards could seem woefully inadequate. In 1909, when he was fifty-one years old, he said: 'My immortal works (13 in all) have brought me last year something under five pounds in royalties' – though that sum was what remained after the repayment of various debts.[27] Ever since his early days of indebtedness to Uncle Bobrowski, Conrad had displayed a resilient capacity for spending more than he earned. Frequently he depended on loans from friends (Galsworthy, Cunninghame Graham and others), on the forbearance of publishers (particularly William Blackwood and William Heinemann), and on the charity of the British taxpayer. In 1902 the Royal Literary Fund gave him £300; in 1904, the 'Royal Bounty Special Service Fund' donated £500; in 1908 there was a further donation of £200 from the Royal Literary Fund; and in 1910 he was awarded a Civil List pension of £100 per annum – a pension which continued until 1917, when at last he was in a position to renounce it. To put these sums in perspective, we should recall that the wages of one of Conrad's maids totalled just £20 per year.[28] Another financial lifeline was provided by J. B. Pinker, the astute Scot who had become Conrad's literary agent in 1900. Pinker's faith that his client would eventually gain popular success was so great that the agent advanced him enormous sums over the years. In 1905 Pinker agreed to lend him £600 per annum; within two years, in addition to debts to Galsworthy and 'a lot of bills unpaid in Kent', Conrad owed the agent £1,572. The extent of Pinker's gamble can be gauged from the fact that in 1905 Henry Newbolt advised the author to make 'a composition with [the] creditors' – a private bankruptcy. By 1909 his debts totalled £2,250, at a time when the average annual earnings of a doctor were less than £400.[29]

During that major phase, accordingly, there developed a clear bifurcation in Conrad's literary creativity. On the one hand, he struggled to create incisive, taxing and innovatory works. On the other hand, he sought to increase the flow of marketable copy by collaborating with Hueffer in a number of inferior projects: not only *The Inheritors* and *Romance*, but also *The Mirror of the Sea*, a volume of reminiscences which appeared under Conrad's name alone. Literary collaborations may be more productive of quarrels than of masterpieces, and by 1909 Conrad was complaining that Ford's conduct was 'impossible' – 'He is a megalomaniac who imagines that he is managing the Universe'.[30] Nevertheless, Ford's fluency, enthusiasm and entrepreneurial energy had helped to guide Conrad through a particularly stressful phase; his eventual reminiscences were to provide some of the liveliest glimpses of Conrad's personality; and the novel *The Good Soldier* (published in 1915) was to be acclaimed by Graham Greene as a work in which the apprentice had surpassed his master.[31]

After Conrad's major phase from 1897 to 1911, the subsequent years until 1919 constituted a period of transition. It was a double transition: first, while some of the novels and tales of this period are admirable, others give clear evidence of a decline in Conrad's powers; and secondly, there was to be a rapid improvement in Conrad's income. In chronological order, the main publications of this phase are: *'Twixt Land and Sea* (three tales); *A Personal Record*, a volume of autobiographical reminiscence which is generally superior to *The Mirror of the Sea*; *Chance*; *Victory*; *Within the Tides* (a collection of four of his more trivial tales); and *The Shadow-Line*. Of the novels in this sequence, critics usually concur in regarding *The Shadow-Line* as the most successful: once again, as had been the case with 'Falk' and 'The Secret Sharer', memories of his captaincy of the *Otago* had proved fruitful. *Victory* is much more problematic for the critics, some seeing it as one of the Conradian masterpieces, others seeing it as a work flawed by melodramatic crudities and heavy-handed allegorizing. The publication which most crucially affected Conrad's fortunes was, of course, *Chance*, which was serialized in the *New York Herald* in 1912 and appeared in book form (after delays caused by a binders' strike) in January 1914. This novel sold remarkably well in both Britain and the United States. Why this should have happened is not immediately obvious, for *Chance* is certainly not one of Conrad's best novels; nor is it obviously 'popular', for the narrative is unfolded slowly and with elaborate deviousness by means of a complicated sequence of narrators and witnesses. The key to its success is probably the shrewdness with which Conrad and the publishers aimed the work at a *female* readership; for women rather than men (then as now) constituted a large majority of the readers of fiction. The serialization in the *New York Herald* was accompanied by a barrage of publicity, stressing that Conrad had written this new novel with women particularly in mind; and the American publishers of the book, Doubleday, made zealous promotional efforts. Alfred Knopf, a young employee, boldly solicited quotable tributes from prominent celebrities. The novel incorporated a running discussion of feminist matters, which provided considerable topicality at a period when the suffragists had been capturing the headlines with their militant and sometimes violent campaigns; and the main narrative concluded with what, by Conradian standards, was a happy ending, with its inhibited hero and heroine at last experiencing the long-delayed sexual embrace. Reviews were generally laudatory, though not markedly better than for earlier and more radical works like *The Nigger of the 'Narcissus'* or *Under Western Eyes*. Whatever the causes, the great commercial success of *Chance* was timely. Conrad had never stinted himself: he had dressed like a dandy or country squire, owned a succession of expensive motor cars, and moved into gradually larger and more impressive houses; but now, at last, he possessed an income more than adequate to his life-style.

In the closing years of his life, from 1919 to 1924, Conrad produced *The Arrow of Gold*, *The Rescue* (which had begun in 1894), *Notes on Life and Letters* (a collection of essays and occasional pieces) and *The Rover*. Posthumously published volumes would include *Suspense* (an unfinished Napoleonic novel), *Tales of Hearsay* (four minor stories) and *Last Essays*. All four novels of this late phase are disappointing: often slow, prolix and basically conventional in their moral orientation. Conrad, who had once been so radical in ideas and techniques, now seemed to be regressing towards stereotypes and romantic conventionalities.

As his writing lost its bite, however, public adulation approached a crescendo. Film rights brought him thousands of pounds; collectors zealously sought his manuscripts, often paying more for these papers than their texts had originally earned from publishers; and during a visit to the United States in 1923 he was lionized. 'To be aimed at by forty cameras held by forty men that look as if they came in droves is a nerve-shattering experience,' he told his wife. Conrad courteously declined numerous academic honours – and even a knighthood offered by Britain's first Labour Prime Minister, Ramsay MacDonald. He had coveted the Nobel Prize for Literature, but that eluded him. Eventually, in the summer of 1924, at the age of sixty-six, he was felled by a heart attack; and, after a service at the Roman Catholic church of St Thomas, he was buried in a public cemetery at Canterbury.

For a while, his reputation and popularity with both the critics and the general public remained high; and the cinema, by presenting films of *Victory* (1920), *Lord Jim* (1925), *Nostromo* (1926), *Romance* (1927) and *The Rescue* (1929), certainly enabled his fame to reach a far larger audience than he could have imagined possible when he began his literary career. In the 1930s, however, there was some slackening of interest in him as a new generation of writers (including D. H. Lawrence,

James Joyce, Aldous Huxley and W. H. Auden) moved into the foreground of discussion. A strong and enduring revival developed in the period 1945–65: F. R. Leavis's *The Great Tradition*, Albert Guerard's *Conrad the Novelist* and Jocelyn Baines's *Joseph Conrad: A Critical Biography* helped to regenerate interest; and the burgeoning of higher education in Europe and North America gave new energy to the 'Conrad industry' of scholarly research and critical appreciation. There came full recognition not only of Conrad's originality as a pioneer of literary Modernism but also of his acutely prophetic powers as a philosophical and political sceptic. He was identified as a potent influence on a diversity of writers ranging from Scott Fitzgerald, William Faulkner and Ernest Hemingway to T. S. Eliot and Graham Greene. Numerous Conradian works were adapted for television or cinema: among them *An Outcast of the Islands*, *Lord Jim*, 'The Secret Sharer', 'The Duel' (as *The Duellists*), 'Heart of Darkness' (freely adapted as *Apocalypse Now*), *Victory* (again), *The Secret Agent*, 'Amy Foster', *The Shadow-Line* and – again – *Nostromo*. The tale 'To-morrow' and the novel *Victory* were transformed into operas. Ngugi wa Thiong'o's fine Kenyan novel, *A Grain of Wheat* (1967), adapted to an African setting major elements of the plot and thematic structure of *Under Western Eyes*; and the film version of 'The Duel', directed by Ridley Scott, even spawned a 'novel of the film' (*The Duellists*), written by Gordon Williams, based on the filmscript by Gerald Vaughn-Hughes, and published by Collins in 1977: so Conrad's literary offspring displayed a philoprogenitive tendency to mutate and crossbreed.

Part 3 Sources and Contexts of *Nostromo*

3.1 Genesis and Production

Conrad began work on *Nostromo* around the end of October 1902.[1]
He envisaged it as a short story in 'the "Karain" class'. Both 'Karain'
and the related Malay tale, 'The Lagoon', portrayed a man haunted
by guilt after his infatuation with a woman had led him to betray a
comrade; a similarity which, coupled with Conrad's later remarks
about the source-book *On Many Seas*, suggests that he had originally
planned a work dealing with Nostromo's guilt after a treacherous theft
and sexual infatuation. In January 1903 he told Pinker, his agent, that
the work's length would be about 35,000 words; but by February he
was talking of 'about 85 thou[sand]'. By March he knew that Giorgio
Viola and his daughters would 'take a good space in the book'; in
May he told Cunninghame Graham that though the novel was set in
South America, 'It is however concerned mostly with Italians'; and in
the same month he reported that on the basis of a synopsis, Harper &
Brothers (a company based in New York) had agreed to publish the
book 'of which *not a quarter* yet is written'. By August 1903 the basic
structure of the work had been thought out and 42,000 words furnished, though Conrad was still grossly underestimating the eventual
length: he imagined that the final version would have about 84,000
words, whereas the book would actually have almost 170,000.[2] Pinker
secured serialization in *T.P.'s Weekly*, and the instalments ran from
29 January to 7 October 1904. Well after serialization commenced,
Conrad was still battling to complete the work; 30 August saw the
end, as he reported to John Galsworthy:

Finished! Finished on the 30th in Hope's house in Stanford in Essex, where I had
to take off my brain that seemed to turn to water. For a solid Fortnight I've been
sitting up. And all the time horrible toothache.
 . . . . . Worked all day. In the evening dear Mrs Hope (who is not used to that
sort of thing) gave me four candles and on I went. Finished at 3. Took me another
half-hour to check the numbering of the pages write a letter to P[inker] and so on.
 I had not the heart to write to you that same night nor yet the next day. Wasn't
sure I would survive. But I have survived extremely well. I feel no elation. The
strain has been too great for that.[3]

19

In any case, there was still further writing to be done, since the serial text was to be variously pruned and expanded for the book version, which appeared (with remarkable celerity) on 14 October.

Thus, what had initially been conceived as a short tale dealing with a group of Italian immigrants (Nostromo, Giorgio Viola and Giorgio's family) had developed into an immense and historically panoramic novel worthy of comparison with Tolstoy's *War and Peace*. A similar process of growth was recurrent in the range of Conrad's works. *Lord Jim* had been conceived as a tale rather than a novel; the same was to be true of *The Secret Agent*, *Under Western Eyes* and *Chance*. Even Conrad's first novel, *Almayer's Folly*, developed into a trilogy with the subsequent appearance of *An Outcast of the Islands* and *The Rescue*; while the biography of the fictional Captain Charles Marlow was to extend transtextually from 'Youth' to 'Heart of Darkness', *Lord Jim* and *Chance*, just as the narrator and location of the tale 'Falk' were to reappear in 'The Secret Sharer' and *The Shadow-Line*. Conrad possessed – and was possessed by – a powerfully exploratory, expansive and interconnective imagination. Notwithstanding the singular immensity and splendour of *Nostromo*, the novel can be seen as a culmination of the political preoccupation that had found its earliest expression in *Almayer's Folly* and had been maintained through all the subsequent novels, and many of the tales, prior to 1904; a preoccupation, engendered by the young Conrad's Polish experiences, with imperialism and – an even larger matter – with the price exacted from striving individuals by long-term processes of historical evolution. Conrad is probably the finest political novelist in the English language; and one reason for this is that he could see not only the enormously tentacular extent of the political (affecting conceptions of race, class, gender and selfhood) but also the tragicomic futility of political action when measured against the cold immensities of the greater environment – the mountains and oceans, the starry skies above, the infinity of space and the eternity of time.

In 1917 Conrad wrote an 'Author's Note' for a new edition of *Nostromo*. There he gave his account of the novel's genesis. He said that while sailing in the Gulf of Mexico in 1875 or 1876 he had heard the story of a man who was believed to have stolen a boatload of silver during a South American revolution. The tale lay dormant until, around 1902, Conrad accidentally found in a second-hand-book shop a shabby volume which gave a fuller account of the same incident. The 'impenitent thief' had openly boasted of his exploit, even though he prudently removed only one bar at a time from his hidden board of silver, explaining: '"I must get rich slowly – you understand."' Conrad remarks:

It was only when it dawned upon me that the purloiner of the treasure need not necessarily be a confirmed rogue, that he could be even a man of character, an actor and possibly a victim in the changing scenes of a revolution, it was only then that I had the first vision of a twilight country which was to become the province of Sulaco, with its high shadowy Sierra and its misty Campo .....[4]

To amplify the character of Nostromo, Conrad then drew on his memories of Dominic Cervoni, that proud and intrepid owner of the *Tremolino* with whom he had sailed in the Mediterranean during the Marseille period. As for Antonia Avellanos, she was based on a beautiful and passionately patriotic schoolgirl – 'an uncompromising Puritan of patriotism' – whom Conrad had loved in the days before he left Poland for France.

I was not the only one in love with her; but it was I who had to hear oftenest her scathing criticism of my levities – very much like poor Decoud – or stand the brunt of her austere, unanswerable invective.[5]

There is no good reason to doubt these claims made in the 'Author's Note'. The 'shabby volume' in the second-hand-book shop was eventually identified by scholars (Halverson and Watt) as *On Many Seas: The Life and Exploits of a Yankee Sailor* (1897), a book of reminiscence by H. E. Hamblen under the pseudonym of 'Frederick Benton Williams'.[6] The identification confirms Conrad's account of the adaptation: the original thief was indeed merely a rogue, whereas Nostromo is a living paradox: the 'incorruptible' man who is corrupted, the utterly trustworthy worker who betrays his trust. Again, the researches of Norman Sherry have confirmed the objective existence of Dominic Cervoni and produced external evidence that he was just such a proud, bold and caustic figure as Conrad described, a 'feared leader' who commanded deference and who was certainly deemed to have been involved in smuggling.[7] The Polish original of Antonia Avellanos has not been identified, but this is partly because the sombre history of Poland, entailing the destruction by war of so many records, has placed daunting obstacles in the path of researchers. In *Nostromo* her character is certainly an amalgam, deriving in part from literary and historical sources: among them, Eastwick's *Venezuela*.

In the 'Author's Note', the references to the Polish girl and to Dominic Cervoni both provide broad hints that Martin Decoud stands in a closer biographical relationship to the author than does any other character in the book. Decoud is a gun-runner, as Conrad claimed to have been; he, too, voyages from Europe to South America. Like Conrad, he is keenly intelligent and acutely sceptical. The young Conrad had anticipated Decoud by attempting suicide with a pistol. And Decoud, like his creator, veers between sardonic cynicism and romantic aspirations and affirmations. There is no doubt that in the characterization of Decoud, Conrad was looking back with understanding – a critical understanding – upon his own earlier self.

Conrad's reference to the Polish original of Antonia also makes quite clear the connection between the fictional Costaguana and the historic Poland. The novel speaks of Costaguana in words which Conrad might well have applied to the tragic history of his native land:

The cruel futility of things stood unveiled in the levity and sufferings of that incorrigible people; the cruel futility of lives and of deaths thrown away in the vain endeavour to attain an enduring solution of the problem.

Similarly, when Decoud is speaking:

'We are a wonderful people, but it has always been our fate to be' – he did not say 'robbed,' but added, after a pause – 'exploited!'[8]

As Jocelyn Baines has pointed out, Conrad's strongly ambivalent attitude to Polish aspirations for independence was inevitably bound up with his attitude to his father:

He had seen at first hand one of the tragic consequences of the political agitation which culminated in the 1863 rising; the exile and disillusionment of his father and the premature death of his mother. In fact the situation between Mr and Mrs Gould is analogous to that between Conrad's parents if political action is substituted for material interests; it is particularly emphasised when Conrad says that Gould is haunted by a fixed idea, and 'a man haunted by a fixed idea is insane. He is dangerous even if that idea is an idea of justice; for may he not bring the heaven down pitilessly upon a loved head?' or when Decoud, speaking of Mrs Gould, points to 'some subtle wrong . . . that sentimental unfaithfulness which surrenders her happiness, her life, to the seduction of an idea'.[9]

The 'Author's Note' mentions a couple of the personal encounters which influenced the book; but there were several others. Probably the most important of these was Conrad's friendship with R. B. Cunninghame Graham, which deserves a section to itself.

3.2 R. B. Cunninghame Graham

Conrad had been corresponding with Cunninghame Graham since 1897; the two men also had occasional meetings which confirmed a warm friendship. Cunninghame Graham (1852–1936) was a living paradox of the kind to appeal particularly to Conrad, for he was an aristocratic socialist, a celebrated public figure who passionately supported the cause of the downtrodden while retaining a sceptical, even melancholy, outlook on the world. Known to his friends as 'Don Roberto', he was one of the most picturesque and adventurous figures of his age, a lithe, athletic dandy, three quarters Scottish, one quarter Spanish; the owner of large (if encumbered) estates in Perthshire and Dunbartonshire; a descendant of King Robert the Bruce, and thereby (according to some Scottish historians) the true heir to the British throne. In his early years he had travelled widely in South and Central America, attempting to make his fortune as a cattle-rancher and horse-dealer, and on his return to Britain he had espoused radical politics, entering Parliament as a Liberal member in 1886 but soon revealing himself as the first socialist in the House of Commons. While there, he became a scathing critic of imperialism and capitalism, and advocated the establishment of a Labour Party (he became founder-president of the first in Great Britain, the Scottish Labour Party) as well as proposing free secular education, the nationalization of industry and finance, Home Rule for Scotland and Ireland, militant trade-unionism and the abolition of the House of Lords. A collaborator with Friedrich Engels, William Morris and Keir Hardie, he was jailed for an impetuous rush against the police during the 'Bloody Sunday' demonstration on 13 November 1887. In addition to his globe-trotting and political campaigning, he established a career as a writer of essays, tales, histories and biographies, soon becoming celebrated as a 'writer's writer' for his distinctive ironic, realistic, sceptical and elegiac outlook – 'elegiac' because of his concern to memorialize bygone and forgotten people and places and to lament the depredations inflicted by the modern commercial spirit.[10]

Conrad, in works prior to *Nostromo*, had dealt with locations that his own journeys had made familiar to himself: life on shipboard, in the Malay Archipelago or in the Congo. In *Nostromo*, however, he was choosing a location (South America) that he had only glimpsed. He complained to Cunninghame Graham in 1903, 'I just had a glimpse 25 years ago – a short glance. That is not enough pour bâtir un roman dessus [to build a novel upon].' And to Richard Curle he later remarked that he had gone ashore for about twelve hours at Puerto Cabello and about two and a half to three days at La Guaira – 'and there were a few hours in a few other places on that dreary coast of Ven[ezue]la'.[11] (That account has yet to receive corroboration.) It seems very likely that the new friendship with Cunninghame Graham helped to turn Conrad's attention to the possibilities of a South American location.

Between 1870 and 1877, Cunninghame Graham had travelled extensively in Argentina, Paraguay and Uruguay, with a briefer excursion into Brazil. He had been involved in revolutionary upheavals, and was an eye-witness of the devastation wrought in Paraguay by the campaigns of the dictator Francísco Solano López. In his writings he frequently reminisces about those early experiences, and there is evidence that such reminiscences formed part of his conversations with Conrad. On 23 June 1898 Edward Garnett wrote to him:

Conrad told me you had once assisted at a battle in Paraguay ..... Will your Joss (or that familiar demon that makes you write) not conjure up for you & for us that battle? Or won't you expand that sentence of yours about 'six women to each man in Paraguay' into a moral sketch on Paraguayan manners[?][12]

Furthermore, during the seven years before the appearance of *Nostromo*, many of Graham's articles and letters to the press commented bitterly on the emergence of the United States of America as a new imperialist power during this period of the Spanish–American War and of the secession of Panama from Colombia through the intervention of the United States. Cunninghame Graham's polemics were part of a widespread debate in the British press about the aggressive policies of the North Americans; and this debate may well have encouraged Conrad to expand *Nostromo* from a relatively limited work dealing with Italian immigrants into a large-scale political novel which, among other things, portrays critically the increasing influence of North American capital and ideology in the affairs of South America. The arrival of US warships ensured the Panamanian secession and, thereby, Washington's control of the Panama Canal, which was then under construction; and in the novel, we see that it is the arrival of the US warship *Powhattan* which ensures the secession of Sulaco from Costaguana and thereby safeguards Holroyd's investment in Gould's silver-mine. (The *Powhattan*, incidentally, was a real steam-frigate, commissioned at Norfolk, Virginia, in 1852.)[13]

Two of Cunninghame Graham's histories of the Spanish Conquest of South America, *A Vanished Arcadia* (1901) and *Hernando de Soto* (1903), were read and enjoyed by Conrad shortly before and during the writing of *Nostromo*, and he particularly relished the parallels drawn between the *conquistadores* and the present-day imperialists, as well as Graham's sardonic emphasis on the hypocrisy and futility of the endeavour to found a durable moral order on the basis of 'material interests' and the quest for treasure. Another anticipation of Conrad's themes is provided by Cunninghame Graham's tactical argument that the cruel destruction inflicted personally by the hardy treasure-seekers of the past was possibly no worse (and certainly less extensive) than the devastation caused relatively impersonally by modern emissaries of 'progress'. At the conclusion of *A Vanished Arcadia*, the author laments that, in spite of the humane work of the Jesuits in Paraguay, the Conquest had ruined the lives of the native inhabitants:

The self-created goddess Progress was justified by works, and all the land left barren, waiting the time when factories shall pollute its sky, and render miserable the European emigrants, who, flying from their slavery at home, shall have found it waiting for them in their new paradise beyond the sea.[14]

The very tone anticipates that of the pessimistic prophecies offered, near the end of *Nostromo*, by Dr Monygham and Cardinal-Archbishop Corbelán. If Cunninghame Graham's socialist idealism offered provocation to Conrad, his sombre view of history may well have reinforced his friend's sceptical convictions.

One of the ironies of the friendship was that although Cunninghame Graham would never have endorsed Charles Gould's faith in 'material interests', Conrad certainly used him as a model for Gould. Norman Sherry has observed:

Both are given Spanish names – Don Roberto, Don Carlos; both are remarkable for their flaming hair and moustaches; both have early family connections with the country in a political sense; both met their wives on the continent of Europe; both wives sketch and both wives went on an exhausting tour of a South American country with their respective husbands.[15]

This list of parallels requires some modification, for in the case of Cunninghame Graham and his wife Gabriela, their exhausting tour together had been of Texas and Mexico rather than of 'a South American country'; but the list will also bear extension. We may add, for instance, that Cunninghame Graham, like Charles Gould, was a celebrated *equestrian* figure – a proudly confident horseman. Both men were fluent in Spanish. Next, the marriage of Robert and Gabriela Cunninghame

Graham proved childless, like that of Charles and Emilia Gould. Though they had made their Mexican journey together, increasingly their journeys took them on separate paths. Finally, and most strikingly: in 1894 Cunninghame Graham had prospected for gold in ancient Spanish mine-workings, in the hope that fresh ore could be found and the mines redeveloped; an anticipation of Charles Gould's faith that the ancient mines of Sulaco might once again yield their silver. (Cunninghame Graham was to describe his unsuccessful venture in 'A Page of Pliny', eventually published in the collection entitled *A Hatchment*, 1913.)

When Cunninghame Graham, at the age of twenty-one, was exploring on horseback the rainy wilds of Paraguay, he sent his mother a letter which includes the following remarks:

I slept out in pouring rain every night & had nothing to eat except oranges & mandioca . . . . .

If I had not met a very nice Italian on the Correntino frontier who lent me a gun (of course I had left my rifle in Asuncion when I wanted it) I should have eaten very little meat on the journey. The Italian was a sort of gentleman & had served in the Crimea[;] he spoke English fluently. 'You like glass God damn.'[16]

This 'very nice Italian' was Enrico Clerici, who was to reappear in several autobiographical tales by Cunninghame Graham: 'Cruz Alta', 'The Captive', 'Feast Day at Santa Maria Mayor' and 'The Stationmaster's Horse'. In 'Cruz Alta' (published in *Thirteen Stories*, 1900), the relevant passage is this:

Two days we passed in Ytapua resting our horses, and I renewed my friendship with Enrico Clerici, an Italian, who had served with Garibaldi, and who, three years ago, I had met in the same place and given him a silver ring which he reported galvanized, and was accustomed to lend as a great favour for a specific against rheumatism. He kept a pulperia [i.e. tavern], and being a born fighter, his delight was, when a row occurred (which he styled 'una barulla de Jesu Cristo' ['a Christian affray': 'barulla' is a misprint of 'baruffa']), to clear the place by flinging empty bottles from the bar. A handsome, gentlemanlike man, and terrible with a bottle in his hand, whether as a weapon of offence or for the purposes of drink; withal well educated and no doubt by this time long dead, slain by his favourite weapon, and his place filled by some fat, double-entry Basque or grasping Catalan, or by some portly emigrant from Germany.[17]

In 'The Captive' (first published in 1909, subsequently included in the volume *Hope*, 1910), the reference is as follows:

Spaniards and Frenchmen sat side by side with an Italian, one Enrique Clerici, who had served with Garibaldi in his youth, but now was owner of a *pulperia* that he had named 'The Rose of the South,' and in it hung a picture of his quondam leader, which he referred to as 'my saint.'[18]

Again, in 'Feast Day at Santa Maria Mayor' (in *Brought Forward*, 1916), Clerici appears as a 'tall and sunburnt' tavern-keeper:

and all his conversation ran upon Garibaldi, with whom he had campaigned in his youth, upon Italia Irredenta [Italy Unredeemed], and on the time when anarchy should sanctify mankind by blood, as he said, and bring about the reign of universal brotherhood.[19]

Since the last two passages post-date *Nostromo*, it is just possible that Cunninghame Graham's memories of Clerici have been influenced by the novel; nevertheless, given the broad consistency of Cunninghame Graham's references, it seems far more likely that Graham's recollections of the Italian, doubtless conveyed in his conversations with Conrad, provided the main basis of Conrad's characterization of Giorgio Viola. The connections are obvious and numerous. Clerici is an Italian tavern-keeper in a remote South American state, as is Viola; Clerici meets people of diverse nationalities, as does Viola; both men are handsome veterans, 'gentlemanlike' and courageous; both men formerly served Garibaldi and now revere the memory of Garibaldi as if he were a saint; Clerici, like Viola, has hung on his wall a picture of the former leader; and both are fervent idealists, longing for a united Italy and the era of brotherhood. A curious detail is that both are the recipients of prized silver gifts: Clerici values a silver ring presented by Cunninghame Graham; Viola values the silver spectacles presented by Emilia Gould. Furthermore, Graham's nostalgically pessimistic sense of 'change for the worse' – the sense that when the redoubtable Clerici is dead his place will be taken by some inferior immigrant – anticipates the entropic theme in Conrad's story of Sulaco: the successors of Viola and Avellanos will lack their nobility of idealism.

Cunninghame Graham's contribution to *Nostromo*, then, was varied and substantial. He had ample first-hand knowledge of South and Central America to convey to Conrad both in conversation and by way of his books and magazine articles. He could provide incidental anecdotes, like the '*y dentista*' ('and a dentist') anecdote which Conrad used in Chapter 9 of Part III. (The serial text, though not the book, preserved this Spanish phrase.)[20] He introduced Conrad to Don Santiago Pérez Triana, the Colombian Ambassador, whose rhetorical idealism is echoed by Don José Avellanos and whose corpulent physique is emulated by President-Dictator Ribiera.[21] More important than any of these considerations may be the paradox generated by Graham's political career and his writings. As politician, Graham often expressed a fervent and extreme socialism, an impatience to do away with the whole capitalist system and its manifold injustices: 'There is no other halting-place for Socialists: either they must reject the whole, or swallow all – or not be honest.'[22] Yet, as writer of tales, essays and histories, he often expressed a melancholy sense of the futility of all human striving when measured against the perennial power of death and oblivion, the vastness of space and the silence of eternity. In *Nostromo*, this great paradox of Graham's career receives more eloquent expression than in any one of Graham's own works. Sydney S. Pawling, partner of the publisher William Heinemann, suggested in May 1904 that Conrad and Cunninghame Graham should collaborate on a literary article, but nothing came of this suggestion;[23] nevertheless, to a greater extent than he may have recognized, Robert Bontine Cunninghame Graham had collaborated in the production of Conrad's titanic political novel.

3.3 Memoirs and Histories

3.3.1 *Mémoires de Garibaldi*

On 23 March 1903, Conrad asked Ford to procure for him 'a life of Garibaldi – a picturesque one', perhaps 'existing under the aegis of Dumas the father'. 'Giorgio shall take a good space in the book,' he added.[24]

The *Mémoires de Garibaldi*, translated by Alexandre Dumas the Elder, were evidently forthcoming. Details from these memoirs were used by Conrad when describing Giorgio Viola's campaigns alongside Giuseppe Garibaldi, the Italian patriot who had gained fame in South America as a military commander defending Montevideo (in Uruguay) against the Argentinians; and Viola's austere republicanism reflects closely the ideals for which Garibaldi was famed. In addition, Garibaldi gives a graphic description of the ordeal he suffered when tortured by means of the strappado or *estrapade*: suspended by his wrists, behind his back, from an overhead beam, he refused to betray his helpers to his tormentor, and spat in the officer's face. Conrad was clearly indebted to this passage when depicting the torture (and similar act of defiance) of Hirsch.[25] The memoirs also provided the name Anzani, the reference to an Englishman called Samuel who served Garibaldi at Montevideo, and hints for the character of Hernández. As Norman Sherry has pointed out, Giorgio Viola's proudly leonine appearance may well have been suggested by portraits and descriptions of the Italian hero.[26] A final detail is that when the dying Teresa Viola calls to Nostromo, 'Gian' Battista! Save the children', she is echoing the sentiments of the dying Anita Garibaldi: 'Giuseppe – the children!'[27]

The originality of Conrad's transformative imagination is illustrated by the fact that the circumstances of Garibaldi's torture are transferred, in the novel, to a completely contrasting figure, the abjectly fearful Hirsch, and that the account of Decoud's suffering during his isolation on the Great Isabel also preserves, as a recurrent motif, the image of the strappado:

In the daytime he could look at the silence like a still cord stretched to breaking-point, with his life, his vain life, suspended to it like a weight.[28]

3.3.2 RAMÓN PÁEZ: *Wild Scenes in South America*, 1863

Conrad owned this book, and borrowed from it descriptions of South American flora and fauna. In particular, he drew on Páez's description of the ominous owl called the *ya acabó*, whose cry is supposed to portend 'calamity or death, ... and is therefore looked upon with dread even by men who would not flinch at the sight of the most formidable bull or jaguar'.[29] In Part III, Chapter 8, of the novel, Nostromo wonders whether Teresa Viola may be still alive:

As if in answer to this thought, half of remorse and half of hope, with a soft flutter and oblique flight, a big owl, whose appalling cry: 'Ya-acabo! Ya-acabo! – it is finished; it is finished' – announces calamity and death in the popular belief, drifted vaguely like a large dark ball across his path. In the downfall of all the realities that made his force, he was affected by the superstition, and shuddered slightly. Signora Teresa must have died, then. It could mean nothing else. The cry of the ill-omened bird, the first sound he was to hear on his return, was a fitting welcome for his betrayed individuality.[30]

What, in Páez's account, was merely a description of the bird, became in *Nostromo* a richly ironic and symbolic episode: the owl's cry is taken by Nostromo to mean that Teresa is dead; but what has perished is also his own career as a man of integrity. Similarly, Páez's description of the '*Rey-Zamuro*, or king of the vultures,' was followed closely by Conrad when depicting the brightly coloured vulture which expectantly attends the sleeping Nostromo; and the new context lends symbolic resonance by associating the man with a fall into disillusioning and possibly mortal knowledge.[31]

Other details of *Wild Scenes* which Conrad may have noted were the reference to the battle of Carabobo (a battle cited in the novel), and numerous Spanish terms which also reappear in Conrad's text: among them, *llaneros* (plainsmen), *blanco* (aristocrat or gentleman), *pulpería* (tavern), *lazos* (lassos), *hato* (cattle-ranch: hence Conrad's place-name 'Los Hatos'), *trabuco* (blunderbuss) and *vaqueros* (cowboys).

3.3.3 E. B. EASTWICK: *Venezuela*, 1868

This book proffered various names: Higuerota, Calle de la Constitución, Páramos (barren icy uplands: hence 'Paramo of Ivie'), *mozo*, Guzmán Blanco (suggesting 'Guzman Bento'), Ribera (suggesting 'Ribiera'), Rincón (corner, nook or narrow valley, and also the name of a country house) and Amarilla (the colour yellow as emblem of a political party); and its description of Puerto Cabello provided a basis for Conrad's account of Sulaco harbour and the Golfo Plácido beyond. The novel's cruel and avaricious Colonel Sotillo was based, in part, on a similarly cruel and avaricious General Sotillo mentioned by Eastwick. The central area of Conrad's Sulaco closely resembles the centre of Caracas in Eastwick's depiction: a large plaza, government buildings on the western side, and a cathedral 'at the south-eastern angle'. Eastwick reminisces about the 'reigning beauty' of Valencia, Antonia Ribera, a Europeanized, well-educated, emancipated young woman with blue eyes and rich brown hair, who was said to desire marriage to nobody unless a foreigner. Evidently Antonia Ribera was one literary progenitor of Antonia Avellanos. Another was the beautiful Erminia, whose devotion to her sick father is noted in *Venezuela*.

The Venezuelan army, Eastwick says, included:

lean old scarecrows and starveling boys not five feet high, the greater number half naked, with huge strips of raw beef twisted round their hats or hanging from their belts.

When depicting Pedrito Montero's followers, Conrad, avid for unexpected and therefore vivid detail, pounced on the beef; his version is:

Emaciated greybeards rode by the side of lean dark youths, marked by all the hardship of campaigning, with strips of raw beef twined round the crowns of their hats . . . . .[32]

Some of the more piquant details of political rhetoric in the novel also prove to be historical. Gamacho denounces aristocrats as 'Goths and paralytics'; the crowd responds, 'Down with the Oligarchs!' In *Venezuela*, it is reported that members of the aristocratic party in Caracas were denounced as 'the Godos and the Epilepticos, the "Goths" and "Epileptics"', and that the crowd shouted 'Down with the oligarchs!'[33]

Eastwick also recalls an embarrassing incident at a banquet, when the Venezuelan President toasted him with the tactless words: 'I drink to the gentleman who has brought us thirty thousand pounds.' Conrad magnifies this incident in Part I, Chapter 8, when General Montero says: 'I drink to the health of the man who brings us a million and a half of pounds.'[34] As this borrowing indicates, there was plenty of material in *Venezuela* to provide Conrad with thematic reflections. Eastwick had travelled from London to South America to negotiate a loan sought by the Venezuelan government, which faced economic difficulties as a consequence of the political turbulence of the region and the financial irresponsibility of previous regimes. (Eastwick himself was clearly a model for Sir John, the novel's financier.) At the embarrassing banquet, one of the speakers

assured us that, as all obstacles to perfect freedom were at length removed, Venezuela would now enjoy permanent tranquillity, during which all the blessings of the golden age would be restored.

Eastwick comments drily:

Ten days afterwards, one of the ministers and a number of leading men were arrested and thrown into prison, while, at the same time, an insurrection with which it was supposed they were connected, broke out in several of the provinces.[35]

Conrad's account of the turbulent past of the San Tomé mine may have been suggested, in part, by Eastwick's remarks on the copper-mines of Aroa:

These mines were worked for a time under the superintendence of Englishmen with good results; but unfortunately one fine day the native miners took it into their heads that they had a grievance against the foreigners, so they fell on them suddenly, split their skulls with hatchets, and decamped with their property. For this cruel and cowardly deed some of the guilty parties were afterwards executed, but the mines were for a time abandoned, and the working of them only lately resumed.[36]

Venezuela also anticipates a major Conradian theme in its comments on La Guaira:

[T]he town, perched on a little rim of shore, at the foot of a tremendous peak,

31

seems like a world's finger-post pointing to the littleness of man and the greatness of nature.[37]

In short, Eastwick's pages provided not only local historical and topographical material, and hints for characterization, but also the basis for an ironic survey of the problems of a South American state: a state potentially wealthy but bedevilled by endemic instability, in a region where the human strife seems to be mocked by the serene majesty of the natural background.

3.3.4 G. F. MASTERMAN: *Seven Eventful Years in Paraguay*, 1869

This offered many names of people, places and objects: Don Carlos Decoud, Mitchell, Gould, Barrios, Corbelán, Captain Fidanza, the 'gomba' (i.e. *gombo*, large drum), yerba maté (tea drunk from a gourd), *morenita* (young brunette), 'a *peyne-de-oro*, or gold comb, [which] now means a woman of the lower class', the Blancos, and 'the Cerro Santo Tomás, a bold square mountain' (equivalent to the square San Tomé mountain in *Nostromo*). 'Marochetti' (a sculptor) reappears as 'Parrochetti' in the novel. Even the phrase 'Gran bestia' ('Great beast') as a term of abuse derives from Masterman's pages. The parrot which, in the novel, cries 'Viva Costaguana' is clearly the offspring of the parrot which, in *Seven Eventful Years*, cries 'Viva Pedro Segundo'.[38]

Masterman himself was a physician and surgeon, 'Chief Military Apothecary, General Hospital, Asuncion, Paraguay'. He worked there during the time of the war with Brazil, when Paraguay was led by the ruthless tyrant, Francísco Solano López. His account of López, who had resided in Paris before returning to South America, provided hints for Conrad's presentation of Pedrito Montero. Masterman was twice arrested and endured long periods of harsh captivity, his ankles fettered; and he was tortured ruthlessly by priests who sought to make him confess to conspiracy against the dictator. In the novel, the torturing of Dr Monygham and other victims by the sadistic priest, Father Berón, was clearly suggested by Masterman's account of his own sufferings at the hands of (among others) Padre Román, who, like the fictional Berón, wore lieutenant's uniform with a small cross embroidered on his left breast. In the serial version of *Nostromo*, the priest's name appears not as Berón but as 'Maiz', and 'Maiz' also derives from Masterman.[39]

Seven Eventful Years gives the following illustration of the ignorance of the populace:

The [River] Paraguay is the standard for position and distance . . . . . They

imagined that it reached to Europe, and could never realize existence of another
continent with an ocean rolling between . . . . . They always confounded London
with England; and even Father Romàn, who had quite an extensive library . . . . .,
asked me, with a most puzzled expression on his face, if Londrès were in
Inglaterra, or Inglaterra in Londrès, and if the latter really adjoined France!

Conrad's equivalent is this:

[W]hen once an inquisitive spirit desired to know in what direction this Europe
was situated, whether up or down the coast, Father Roman, to conceal his
perplexity, became very reserved and severe. 'No doubt it is extremely far away.
But ignorant sinners like you of the San Tomé mine should think earnestly of
everlasting punishment instead of inquiring into the magnitude of the earth, with
its countries and populations altogether beyond your understanding.'[40]

Again, Masterman comments on López's use of the books in the
public library at Asunción:

Lopez found, however, a most characteristic use for them: he had the ponderous
tomes cut up for rocket and squib cases! I saw them once serving thus a folio
Hebrew Bible, with an interleaved Latin translation – a most South American
mode of diffusing useful knowledge.

Conrad offers a related account of the treatment of Don José Avellanos's
History of Fifty Years of Misrule:

'[H]asn't he seen the sheets of "Fifty Years of Misrule," which we have begun
printing on the presses of the *Porvenir*, littering the Plaza, floating in the gutters,
fired out as wads for trabucos loaded with handfuls of type, blown in the wind,
trampled in the mud? I have seen pages floating upon the very waters of the harbour.'[41]

An important theme of *Nostromo* is anticipated at the end of Masterman's book, when Masterman says that although the depredations of
Paraguay will eventually give way to an era of commercial prosperity, he
retains some nostalgia for 'the picturesque beauties' of the past.

3.3.5 RICHARD F. BURTON: *Letters from the Battle-Fields of Paraguay*, 1870

Burton's account of Dr Francia, Dictator of Paraguay, emphasizes his
infatuation with books about 'the French Republic, the Consulate, and
the Empire' and says that he 'dreamed in early days of becoming
Consul, Dictator, and Imperator'; thus it anticipates Conrad's presentation of Pedrito Montero.[42] Burton also refers to 'D[on] Juan Decoud',
editor of a Liberal newspaper, who was obliged to flee from Paraguay in

order to escape the vengeful wrath of Francísco Solano López. Other names which reappear in *Nostromo* include Gould and Rincón.[43]

When we look back over this range of source-books dealing with South American history, we may well be impressed not only by the extent and diligence of Conrad's research for *Nostromo*, but also by Conrad's astonishing ability to assimilate and coordinate thematically so many disparate items, frequently giving to borrowed details a richness of symbolic significance which, predictably, they lacked in their original non-fictional settings. Another impressive feature is the extent to which *Nostromo*'s depiction of South American history, even in its more grotesque, ludicrous or tragicomic aspects, is authenticated by the documentary materials. Naturally, some of these accounts reflect the attitudes of a dismayed or disenchanted British observer; but South American assessments of the careers of ruthless leaders like Dr Francia or Francísco Solano López, coupled with the autobiographical works of eminent figures like José Antonio Páez and Santiago Pérez Triana, amply justify the central emphasis on the devastating post-colonial turmoil which, for so much of the nineteenth century (and for too much of the twentieth), was the most conspicuous feature of political life in many South American republics.

3.4 French Literature

It is characteristic of Conrad's linguistic cosmopolitanism that when he referred to himself as *homo duplex* (the double man), he was using a Latin phrase that he had read in Flaubert's *Bouvard et Pécuchet*.[44] Conrad's essays and correspondence make evident his admiration for three celebrated French writers: Gustave Flaubert (1821–80), Guy de Maupassant (1850–93) and Anatole France (1844–1922). Flaubert provided a model of priestly dedication to literary art, the self-sacrificing quest for the precise word, *le mot juste*. He had striven for cool lucidity in seeing life as it is, warts and all; in *Madame Bovary* he brought a new scrupulous diligence of attention to ostensibly mediocre lives in mediocre settings. A related realism was one of Maupassant's strengths: the unshockable rendering of sexual infidelities and the manifold deceptions and betrayals in urban or rural life. And in Anatole France, who became celebrated for his anti-clerical satire *L'Île des pingouins*, Conrad found a third master of sceptical realism and dry irony. It is as though, to counterbalance the lyrical romanticism which was so potent a feature of

Polish literature, Conrad needed models of poised, sophisticated, urbanely controlled writing.

Numerous passages in Conrad's work bring these three French novelists and story-tellers to mind. Sometimes the reason is a temperamental affinity: like them, Conrad had a keen sense of human isolation and of the disparity between romantic aspirations and mundane achievements; like them, he was well aware of strivings mocked by circumstances. Increasingly, however, critics and scholars have adduced textual similarities which indicate that Conrad, whether deliberately or accidentally, often borrowed specific phrases from his French mentors.[45] (Sometimes he may have repeated phrases without recalling their source.) There is no doubt, for example, that certain details of *The Nigger of the 'Narcissus'* derive from Maupassant's novel *Bel-Ami*, while the characterization of Alice in 'A Smile of Fortune' is indebted to the same author's tale, 'Les Sœurs Rondoli'.[46]

In the case of *Nostromo*, the following parallels have been adduced by commentators. When Decoud is close to death, the narrator says of him:

What should he regret? He had recognised no other virtue than intelligence, and had erected passions into duties . . . . . His sadness was the sadness of a sceptical mind. He beheld the universe as a succession of incomprehensible images . . . . .

A victim of the disillusioned weariness which is the retribution meted out to intellectual audacity, the brilliant Don Martin Decoud . . . . . disappeared without a trace.

The phrasing indubitably echoes that of Anatole France's essay, 'Mérimée':

De quoi se serait il repenti? Il ne reconnut jamais pour vertus que les énergies ni pour devoirs que les passions. Sa tristesse n'était-elle pas plutôt celle du sceptique pour qui l'univers n'est qu'une suite d'images incompréhensibles . . . . .? Enfin, n'éprouvait-il pas cette amertume de l'esprit et du cœur, châtiment inévitable de l'audace intellectuelle . . . . .? [What should he regret? He had never recognized anything but energy as virtue or anything but passions as duties. Was not his sadness rather that of the sceptic for whom the universe is only a succession of incomprehensible images . . . . .? Eventually, did he not suffer that bitterness of spirit and heart, the inevitable retribution for intellectual audacity . . . . .?][47]

From the same essay probably derives Decoud's lack of belief 'in the possibility of friendship existing between man and woman'.[48]

An earlier detail in the presentation of Decoud echoes Flaubert's *L'Éducation sentimentale*. There the narrator says of Madame Arnoud's effect on Frédéric:

toutes les femmes lui rappelaient celle-là, par des similitudes ou par des contrastes violentes . . . . .
[all women recalled to him that one, by some similarities or by some violent contrasts . . . . .]

Of Decoud, we are told:

all the girl friends of his sisters recalled to him Antonia Avellanos by some faint resemblance, or by the great force of contrast . . . . .[49]

Yves Hervouet has suggested that the scene in which Decoud and Antonia talk alone on the balcony, screened from the other guests, has various features in common with a love-scene in Maupassant's tale 'L'Héritage' (in both, the lovers lean side by side, their elbows touching, now silent, now conversing), and that Nostromo's love-relationship with Giselle has parallels in *Bel-Ami.*[50] Some of the postulated connections are tenuous, however, and may derive simply from a common stock of romantic phraseology: 'She fascinated him', 'seductive voice', 'heaving of the breast', etc. When, however, Nostromo murmurs caressingly to Giselle as though she were a frightened child, and calls her 'his star and his little flower', the phrasing clearly derives from Anatole France's description in *Balthasar* of King Balthasar's encounter with Balkis: he, too, speaks caressingly, as nurses address children, and '*Il l'appela sa petite fleur et sa petite étoile*' ['He called her his little flower and his little star'].[51] An even clearer instance of indebtedness is the following depiction of Linda Viola:

Linda pouted, advanced her red lips, which were almost too red; but she had admirable eyes, brown, with a sparkle of gold in the irises, full of intelligence and meaning, and so clear that they seemed to throw a glow upon her thin, colourless face.

In Flaubert's *L'Éducation sentimentale*, Mademoiselle Vatnaz is described as follows when she converses with Arnoux:

Et elle lui faisait la moue, en avançant ses grosses lèvres, presque sanguinolentes à force d'être rouges. Mais elle avait d'admirables yeux, fauves avec des points d'or dans les prunelles, tout pleins d'esprit, d'amour et de sensualité. Ils éclairaient, comme des lampes, le teint un peu jaune de sa figure maigre.
[And she pouted, advancing her full lips, which looked almost bloodily red. But she had admirable eyes, fawn, with specks of gold in the irises, full of spirit, love and sensuality. They illuminated, like lamps, the somewhat yellow hue of her thin face.][52]

Elsewhere in *Nostromo*, the narrator offers these important generalizations:

Only in the conduct of our action can we find the sense of mastery over the Fates
. . . . .

In our activity alone do we find the sustaining illusion of an independent existence . . . . .

These claims appear to derive from the discussion of work in Anatole France's *L'Anneau d'améthyste*:

Nous nous flattons d'entreprendre par lui sur les destins . . . . . Le travail nous donne l'illusion de la volonté, de la force et de l'indépendance.
[We flatter ourselves that by means of it we achieve mastery over the Fates . . . . . Work gives us the illusion of will-power, strength and independence.][53]

From the same volume derive Pedrito Montero's interest in the writing of Imbert de Saint-Amand and his admiration for the duc de Morny: France's Maurice Cheiral reads with enthusiasm '*un livre de M. Imbert de Saint-Amand*' and wishes for a life of pleasure like that led by '*le duc de Morny*'.[54] Mrs Gould, too, seems to be prompted by Anatole France when she reflects that

for life to be large and full, it must contain the care of the past and of the future in every passing moment of the present. Our daily work must be done to the glory of the dead, and for the good of those who come after.

In *Le Lys rouge*, a poetess says to a sculptor:

Monsieur Dechartre, pour que la vie soit grande et pleine, il faut y mettre le passé et l'avenir. Nos œuvres . . . . ., il faut les accomplir en l'honneur des morts, et dans la pensée de ceux qui naîtront.
[Monsieur Dechartre, for life to be great and full, one must include in it the past and the future. Our works . . . . . must be accomplished in honour of the dead and with thought for those who are yet to be born.][55]

Even when Conrad, in his 'Author's Note', says that *Nostromo* deals with 'the passions of men short-sighted in good and evil', he may be echoing the opinion of Anatole France's Abbé Coignard that men are '*également médiocres dans le mal comme dans le bien*' ('equally mediocre in evil and good').[56]

As Shakespeare took ideas and phrases from Plutarch and Holinshed, seizing and re-animating, so Conrad used his French mentors; and, rather as in Shakespeare's case, the resultant passages are often charged with greater intensity and a wider significance than had been formerly present. The transformative effects of the new fictional contexts usually redeem Conrad from the imputation of plagiarism. It should now be

evident, however, that Conrad's breadth of vision is related to a remarkable breadth of retentive reading. He became domiciled in England and
wrote his novels in English; but culturally he remained an inter-
nationalist.

3.5 Newspapers and Periodicals

In the decade before the publication of *Nostromo*, work by Conrad had
been published in the magazines *Cosmopolis, Outlook, Illustrated London
News, Pall Mall, Blackwood's, Savoy* and *The New Review*; he appears to
have subscribed to *The Times*, and was an avid reader of *The Saturday
Review* (which published material by various acquaintances of his: Cunninghame Graham, Shaw and Wells). Anyone who browses among such
periodicals soon discovers the prominence, at the time, of the debate
about economic and martial imperialism. *The Times* (5 May 1898, p. 7)
reported a topical speech by the British Prime Minister, Lord Salisbury:

From the necessities of politics or under the pretence of philanthropy – the living
nations will gradually encroach on the territory of the dying . . . . . It is not to be
supposed that any one nation of the living nations will be allowed to have the
profitable monopoly of curing or cutting up these unfortunate patients (laughter)
. . . . . We shall not allow England to be at a disadvantage in any re-arrangement.

As this speech indicates, Great Britain was finding that her vast power
was being challenged by new rivals, particularly by the United States
and Germany. In the same period, the Boer War made clear the heavy
price exacted by British penetration of Africa: 'I should think Lord
Salisbury's dying nation must be enjoying the fun,' remarked Conrad
sardonically.[57] Central and South American affairs also figured promi-
nently in the news, particularly in 1898, when Spain was defeated in war
by the United States, losing Puerto Rico, Cuba and the Philippines.
Conrad commented thus on the Spanish–American War:

It is a miserable affair whichever way you look at it. The ruffianism on one side,
an unavoidable fate on the other, the impotence on both sides, though from
various causes, all this makes a melancholy and ridiculous spectacle. Will the
certain issue of that struggle awaken the Latin race to the sense of its dangerous
position? Will it be any good if they did awaken? . . . . . But, perhaps, the race is
doomed? It would be a pity. It would narrow life, it would destroy a whole side of
it which had its morality and was always picturesque and at times inspiring. The
others may well shout Fiat lux! [Let there be light!] It will be only the reflected
light of a silver dollar and no sanctimonious pretence will make it resemble the

Sources and Contexts of Nostromo

real sunshine . . . . . [M]en are 'fourbes lâches, menteurs, voleurs, cruels' ['mean cheats, liars, thieves, cruel people'] and why one should show a preference for one manner of displaying these qualities rather than for another passes my comprehension in my meditative moments.[58]

(His mixture of partisanship and sceptical detachment anticipates Decoud's response to Costaguanan politics.) Reports of Panama's secession from Colombia provoked from Conrad the sardonic query to Cunninghame Graham: 'And à propos what do you think of the Yankee Conquistadores in Panama? Pretty, isn't it?'[59] The turbulent unrest in the unstable South American republics (and the perils of investment in them) had often enough, in the mid to late nineteenth century, been a topic of regretful comment in the British papers; prominent coverage had been given to the war between Chile, Peru and Bolivia over the Atacama nitrate fields (1879–84), the war mentioned in *Nostromo*, Part I, Chapter 6. One of the keynotes of the novel is provided by the recurrent phrase 'material interests', and this phrase was a cliché of political debates in the press. On 24 February 1900, for example, the Liberal magazine *The Speaker*, which subsequently published articles by Conrad, contained an item by George Russell (entitled 'The Revival of Imperialism') which declared: 'Today . . . . . We see lust of territory, lust of gold, lust of blood; the idolatry of material interests; the shameless repudiation of all moral appeals . . . . .'[60]

If we turn from *Nostromo*'s themes to its plot, we find that one apparently implausible detail may have been suggested by a newspaper item. In Part II, Chapter 8, the lighter carrying the silver, Nostromo, Decoud and Hirsch collides with Sotillo's troop-ship. Hirsch vanishes from the lighter during the collision, and Nostromo thinks he has drowned; but Hirsch reaches shore as a prisoner, having amazingly transferred himself to the larger vessel during the moments of contact. (This unlikely transference is crucial to the plot, for Hirsch then alerts Sotillo to the presence of the cargo of silver.) At the end of January 1898, the British ship *Ardoe* collided in the English Channel with a French ship named (according to a reporter) the *Burgese Strasbourg*; the *Ardoe* had to be beached to prevent her sinking, and her steward vanished during the collision and was presumed drowned; but, remarkably, when the other vessel limped into Dunkirk, *The Times* was able to report that 'She had on board the missing steward of the *Ardoe*, who climbed on board the French ship when the two vessels were in contact.' (*The Times*, 2 February 1898, p. 7)

3.6 Evolutionary History

One of the dominant preoccupations of the century and a half before the appearance of *Nostromo* was undoubtedly evolution, whether in the realms of geology, biology, history or politics. Charles Darwin's *Origin of Species* (1859) was part of a trend: Darwin avowed his indebtedness to Malthus's theory of population and to Sir Charles Lyell's *Principles of Geology* (1830–33). Tennyson's *In Memoriam*, which grapples at great length with the enormity of the moral and theological problems presented by the principles of evolution, antedates *The Origin of Species* and was, in part, prompted by Lyell's work. Tennyson reflected:

> Are God and Nature then at strife,
>   That Nature lends such evil dreams?
>   So careful of the type she seems,
> So careless of the single life . . . . .
>
> 'So careful of the type?' but no.
>   From scarped cliff and quarried stone
>   She cries, 'A thousand types are gone;
> I care for nothing, all shall go.
>
> 'Thou makest thine appeal to me.
>   I bring to life, I bring to death;
>   The spirit does but mean the breath:
> I know no more.' And he, shall he,
>
> Man, her last work, who seem'd so fair,
>   Such splendid purpose in his eyes,
>   Who roll'd the psalm to wintry skies,
> Who built him fanes of fruitless prayer,
>
> Who trusted God was love indeed
>   And love Creation's final law –
>   Tho' Nature, red in tooth and claw
> With ravine, shriek'd against his creed –
>
> Who lov'd, who suffer'd countless ills,
>   Who battled for the True, the Just,
>   Be blown about the desert dust,
> Or seal'd within the iron hills?[61]

As the poem so vividly shows, one effect of the scientific theories of evolution was to challenge or subvert the faith of Christians. The evolutionists' account of the origin of man contrasted with the biblical account, and there was a gross disparity between the vast impersonal forces invoked by Lyell or Darwin and the traditional concept of a God who takes a very personal interest in the individual soul. A related effect was to diminish humans, for they could seem dwarfed by the colossal time-scale of global evolution, as also by the immensity of the solar systems increasingly revealed by astronomy. In the works of Conrad, as in those of his contemporary, Thomas Hardy, one source of creative energy and irony is the imaginative contrast between, on the one hand, the importance that human beings customarily attribute to their individual selves, and, on the other hand, the ephemeral pettiness of human beings when contrasted with the enduring lifeless immensities of time and space. One irony, of course, is that man is both blessed and cursed by knowledge: alone among the animal kingdom, the human being has the knowledge to perceive the vast extent of his environment; yet that same knowledge may bring the sense of 'irremediable littleness', as Conrad termed it.

Historians' attempts to detect an evolutionary pattern in human endeavours had diverse consequences. Adam Smith, in *The Wealth of Nations* (1776), had long ago drawn attention to the fact that economic evolution follows its own predictable and inexorable course: individuals may have a diversity of motives and conflicting ambitions, but the total effect of their strivings for economic advancement is to fulfil certain laws: an 'invisible hand' operates. He claimed that in Scotland the clan system, whereby a chieftain who maintained his loyal supporters could make war on his neighbours and even against the king, had been destroyed not by legal edicts but by commerce:

what all the violence of the feudal institutions could never have effected, the silent and insensible operation of foreign commerce and manufactures gradually brought about. These gradually furnished the great proprietors with something for which they could exchange the whole surplus produce of their lands, and which they could consume themselves without sharing it either with tenants or retainers. All for ourselves and nothing for other people, seems, in every age of the world, to have been the vile maxim of the masters of mankind.[62]

Nevertheless, he argued, the effect of commercial self-interest has been to establish civilized society.

The increase and riches of commercial and manufacturing towns, contributed to the improvement and cultivation of the countries to which they belonged in three different ways.

First, by affording a ready and great market for the rude produce of the

country, they gave encouragement to its cultivation and further improvement
.....

Secondly, the wealth acquired by the inhabitants of cities was frequently employed in purchasing such lands as were to be sold, of which a great part would frequently be uncultivated .....

Thirdly, and lastly, commerce and manufactures gradually introduced order and good government, and with them, the liberty and security of individuals, among the inhabitants of the country, who had before lived almost in a continual state of war with their neighbours, and of servile dependency upon their superiors.[63]

Some parts of Smith's case recall the thesis of Bernard Mandeville in *The Fable of the Bees* (1714): 'Private Vices, Publick Benefits': by pursuing our selfish interests we cannot help but contribute to the general good, for even the magnate who seeks to aggrandize solely himself must still pay the wages of servants, labourers, architects, artists. In turn, the wide dissemination of Smith's thesis has clearly influenced the thinking of Gould in *Nostromo*, who so firmly believes that only if the material interests gain a firm footing in Costaguana can there be a durable basis for peace and prosperity. Smith's ideas helped to nourish the 'Whig View' of history, which was greatly influential in the nineteenth century: an optimistic, teleological view of inevitable, if gradual, progress towards an enlightened, civilized era. Hence, Macaulay's *History of England* (1848–61) attacked the Romantic cult of nostalgia for the past:

In every experimental science there is a tendency towards perfection. In every human being there is a wish to ameliorate his own condition. These two principles have often sufficed, even when counteracted by great public calamities and by bad institutions, to carry civilisation rapidly forward .....

It is now the fashion to place the golden age of England in times when noblemen were desitute [*sic*] of comforts the want of which would be intolerable to a modern footman, when farmers and shopkeepers breakfasted on loaves the very sight of which would raise a riot in a modern workhouse ..... It may well be, in the twentieth century, that the peasant of Dorsetshire may think himself miserably paid with fifteen shillings a week; that the carpenter at Greenwich may receive ten shillings a day; that labouring men may be as little used to dine without meat as they now are to eat rye bread; that sanitary police [*sic*] and medical discoveries may have added several more years to the average length of human life .....[64]

Meanwhile, Macaulay's contemporary, Karl Marx, had formulated a view of economic evolution which drew upon, but contrasted with, Adam Smith's. In the Marx–Engels *Communist Manifesto* (1848), the notion of the inexorable working of economic laws was retained; the new development was the emphasis on class strife. In Marx's scheme, the feudal economic system inevitably gives way to the era of mercantilism and capitalism; for a while the bourgeoisie is the progressive and revolutionary force; but the capitalist system in turn generates the conditions for its own destruction by creating a discontented and increasingly militant proletariat, which eventually (inevitably) seizes power and establishes its dictatorship whereby to inaugurate the era in which equality prevails and class conflict is at last annulled. Conrad was amply familiar with socialist and Marxist theories, partly from his reading (which included such periodicals as H. M. Hyndman's Marxist *Social-Democrat* and Keir Hardie's *Labour Leader*) and partly from his discussions with left-wing friends like Cunninghame Graham (who shared platforms with Engels) and Edward Garnett.

Nostromo can thus be seen as a novel in which rival concepts of historical evolution are put to the test. Gould's theories tally well with Adam Smith's; Captain Mitchell's eventual view has resemblances to Macaulay's; and both are criticized by an emphasis on emergent class-strife in Sulaco which might well gratify a Marxist reader (and has indeed gratified some Marxist critics). But Conrad then puts Marxism in a critical perspective by his pejorative but historically astute depiction of the Marxist photographer who watches at the bedside of the dying 'man of the people'.

Nostromo's general scepticism about progress based on 'material interests' (epitomized in Dr Monygham's claim that only 'a moral principle' can sustain lasting stability) may have been reinforced by Conrad's familiarity with the writings of Carlyle and Dickens. Thomas Carlyle, in 'Chartism' (1839), denounced 'epochs when Cash Payment has become the sole nexus of man to man'; and, in 'Corn-Law Rhymes' (1832), he had declared that 'all Reform except a moral one will prove unavailing'.[65] Among the literary ancestors of Charles Gould is Dickens's Mr Dombey in *Dombey and Son*: a wealthy businessman whose concern for his firm resembles a monomania which alienates him from his wife and daughter. But Dickens's relatively theatrical treatment, which concludes with a maudlin consolatory victory for familial affection, emphasizes by contrast not only Conrad's bleaker outlook but also Conrad's wider vision in space and time. Like Thomas Hardy, Joseph Conrad could, in some moods, see humanity as a conscious incongruity in the evolutionary scheme. As he remarked to Cunninghame Graham: 'What makes mankind tragic is not that they are the victims of nature, it is that they are conscious of it'; 'The fate of a humanity condemned ultimately to perish from cold is not worth troubling about.'[66]

3.7 Determinism, Quixotism, Solipsism and Language

In the nineteenth century, science enjoyed enormous prestige. Today, we are more aware that scientific laws change from age to age, and that scientific fact in one period may be fantasy in another. In the Middle Ages, it was 'scientific fact' that the sun went round the earth; but the cosmology of Ptolemy has been superseded by that of Copernicus, and Newton has been superseded by Einstein. Although there has, on the whole, been an accumulation of valid knowledge about the universe, it is also the case that what often seemed to be a great advance in science was a reorientation of the known facts so as to suit the changing values of society. We are also far more aware that a scientist's conclusions are implicit in his premises; that he can see only what his circumstances enable him to see; and that his researches may help to support oppressive political systems.

When Conrad was a young man, however, science seemed to be making vast progress in many areas – astronomy, geology, biology, physics, engineering; and the burgeoning of European industrial technology was transforming Europe and changing the world. New weapons, new machines, new means of transport; and, dominating a largely submissive globe, a thriving and expanding 'workshop of the world'. Here, in the spectacular advances of the capitalist economies, lay some of the reasons both for the prestige of science and for the notion that it was unfailingly 'objective'.

Some scientific 'laws' are analytic propositions, or deductions from them; and often they resemble tautologies, being the agreed rules of a useful game rather than facts inherent in the observable world. (An example is the law that in normal conditions water freezes at zero degree centigrade.) Many other scientific 'laws' are synthetic propositions, or inductions: they are generalizations inferred from a number of experimental observations. These are not rigid, binding, permanent laws: they are potentially refutable and may be revised, corrected or scrapped in the light of further observations: they are generalizations by people and are not things built into the physical world. Again, though event is linked to event by a sequence of cause and effect, that sequence is not a binding, compelling sequence. I sit here now because a bus has brought me from the station, but the causal sequence has not been a determined or determining one: events could have happened otherwise: the train or bus might have been cancelled.

In the nineteenth century, causality was often confused with determinism; and, consequently, various writers expressed, if only intermittently, the pessimistic sense that free will was an illusion, since science could, apparently, trace the laws governing our every moment. An inconstant but powerful sense of the universe as a soulless mechanism is one source of Conrad's pessimism, as the following words to Cunninghame Graham indicate:

> There is a – let us say – a machine. It evolved itself (I am severely scientific) out of a chaos of scraps of iron and behold! – it knits. I am horrified at the horrible work and stand appalled. I feel it ought to embroider – but it goes on knitting . . . . . And the most withering thought is that the infamous thing has made itself; made itself without thought, without conscience, without foresight, without eyes, without heart. It is a tragic accident – and it has happened. You can't interfere with it . . . . .
>
> It knits us in and it knits us out. It has knitted time space, pain, death, corruption, despair and all the illusions – and nothing matters. I'll admit however that to look at the remorseless process is sometimes amusing.[67]

If 'nothing matters', then man, as a moral being, is superfluous. And one figure who haunts European literature in the nineteenth century is the 'superfluous man'.

He can be found in Russian novels, tales and plays: Pechorin, for instance, the central figure of Lermontov's *A Hero of Our Time*; Tchulkaturin, in Turgenev's 'Diary of a Superfluous Man'; the protagonist of Chekhov's 'A Moscow Hamlet'; and a variety of prominent figures in Chekhov's plays. The most fully developed instance of this type is probably the narrator of Dostoyevsky's *Notes from Underground*. However he looks at his situation, this morbid Hamlet feels himself to be threatened by 'the stone wall' of laws, whether they be those of the utilitarian economists or of evolutionary scientists; men can appear to him 'the keys of a piano, which the laws of nature threaten to control so completely'. He considers various responses to this belittling sense of determinism. One is to be Hamlet-like: to shrug one's shoulders and do nothing, submitting to inertia. (If action is compelled, perhaps inaction manifests, perversely, a sense of independence.) The second way is to assert one's independence by acting in apparent defiance of rational laws: to be quixotic, using one's will wilfully; acting capriciously, even anarchically. '[I]t is just his fantastic dreams, his vulgar folly, that he will desire to retain, simply in order to prove to himself . . . . . that men still are men and not the keys of a piano . . . . .'[68]

From the mid nineteenth century onwards, the accelerating erosion of religious belief reduced the sense that moral standards had absolute objective warrant. One of the numerous cultural consequences was that Cervantes's Don Quixote came to be regarded not just as a lovable literary eccentric but increasingly as a symbol of modern idealism: for his idealism had patently lacked objective sanction. The preoccupation with quixotism probably reached its extreme in 1906, when Miguel de Un-amuno published *Our Lord Don Quixote*, a philosophical and religious commentary which proposed that we adopt Cervantes's deluded knight as the Christ for our times. An earlier sign of this preoccupation was a lecture by Conrad's favourite Russian author, Turgenev. In 'Hamlet and Don Quixote' (1860), Turgenev argued that Hamlet and Don Quixote represent 'the twin antitypes of human nature, the two poles of the axle-tree on which that nature turns': Hamlet is a sceptical egoist, his will paralysed by reflection, whereas Quixote is an active campaigner who can act vigorously, although he is deluded: his giants are merely windmills.[69]

In Conrad's works, this Hamlet/Don Quixote dichotomy is almost alarmingly applicable to a wide range of characters. I say 'almost alarmingly' because this fact suggests a certain schematic ruthlessness about Conrad's patterns of characterization and because we are thus reminded of Conrad's pessimistic emphasis on impotence and futility. Several of his major works, and *Nostromo* in particular, suggest that all conduct governed by pursuit of some ideal is quixotic, both in the sense that it will be betrayed by the facts of harsh actuality ('There was something inherent in the necessities of successful action which carried with it the moral degradation of the idea') and in the sense that the quester may appear deranged in proportion to his degree of devotion to that ideal: '[E]very conviction, as soon as it became effective, turned into that form of dementia the gods sent upon those they wish to destroy'. The narrator observes of Gould:

A man haunted by a fixed idea is insane. He is dangerous even if that idea is an idea of justice; for may he not bring the heaven down pitilessly upon a loved head?

When trying to sum up the political confusions of South America, Decoud says: 'There is a curse of futility upon our character: Don Quixote and Sancho Panza, chivalry and materialism, high-sounding sentiments and a supine morality . . . . .'[70]

In his most sceptical moods, Conrad could regard any and every apparently purposeful action as quixotic. If human beings were the predetermined puppets of causality, in a universe devoid of God, of responsiveness, of ultimate purpose, they all resembled Don Quixote by being futile and deluded, the sense of effective action being only an illusion. The point is uncompromisingly made in the most famous epigram of *Nostromo*, an epigram which deploys dauntingly the words 'illusion' and 'helpless':

In our activity alone do we find the sustaining illusion of an independent existence as against the whole scheme of things of which we form a helpless part.

In an essay on Anatole France, Conrad expressed a similar view:

[H]e wishes us to believe and to hope, preserving in our activity the consoling illusion of power and intelligent purpose.

The theme is repeated in Conrad's 'Autocracy and War':

Action, in which is to be found the illusion of a mastered destiny, can alone satisfy our uneasy vanity and lay to rest the haunting fear of the future . . . . .[71]

If Turgenev's Don Quixote looms large in Conrad's pages, so also does Turgenev's Hamlet. An obvious offspring is *Nostromo*'s Decoud, the sophisticated sceptic who sees the folly of activities that others take seriously (though it should be noted that his scepticism is sometimes surpassed by the narrator's), and who, when isolated on an island, experiences 'the crushing paralysing sense of human littleness', comes to doubt even his own individuality, and eventually shoots himself. A kindred example is Axel Heyst, hero of *Victory*, the victim of his own sceptical reflections: 'The young man learnèd to reflect, which is a destructive process, a reckoning of the cost. It is not the clear-sighted who lead the world.'[72] Generally in Conrad's fiction it is the rule that the more reflective the man, the more likely he is to prove fallible or unreliable in action; and the more stolidly imperceptive the man, the more likely he is to prove resiliently dependable in action. If you wish to ally yourself to one who is consistent and seems designed for survival, you should ally yourself with Sancho Panza or Horatio rather than with their masters. And in Conrad's pages such dependables are represented by Singleton (in *The Nigger of the 'Narcissus'*), MacWhirr ('Typhoon'), the boiler-maker ('Heart of Darkness'), or Don Pepe and Captain Mitchell in *Nostromo*.

One reason for the unreliability of the reflective man is that he may become a victim of solipsism. While determinism is the belief that all things are determined and that free will is therefore an illusion, solipsism is the belief that the individual self constitutes the sole reality. On the one hand, man is the puppet of the universe and its causal laws; on the other, man is a flame of awareness glowing in the midst of a dark flux of the unknown. They are contrasting notions, yet both derive from the prestige of empiricism.

Since the empirical outlook of science has the basic assumption that the foundation of all worthwhile knowledge is the evidence of the senses, recognition that the senses can deceive us may appear to reveal a threat to the basis of all certainty. Since our senses deceive us some of the time (as in optical illusions, in defects of vision or hearing, or in dreams), it is theoretically possible that they can deceive us all the time; in which case we can be certain only of our own existence, it may seem, and of nothing beyond. Common sense revolts against such a notion, though it has long tested the resources of philosophers. We could argue that our faith that the world is substantially as common sense assumes it to be rests not on any naïve belief in the infallibility of the senses but rather on the value-judgement that it is good for our assumptions about the status of the world to be fulfilled. Predictions based on the assumption that the world is as stable as common sense assumes it to be are, in the main, sufficiently fulfilled; while predictions based on the assumption that the world is essentially 'private' or phantasmagoric tend not to be fulfilled. A. J. Ayer's *Foundations of Empirical Knowledge* points out, in addition, that the solipsist's case often seems to thrive on a confusion of terminology:

If we agree to say that the objects of which we are directly aware are always sense-data, then we are deciding to treat them and not minds or material things as the units in terms of which we are to describe our perceptual experience . . . . . [73]

Accordingly, you can describe experience in terms of sense-data (that's one useful convention); or, alternatively, you can describe experience in terms of 'self and world' (that's another useful convention); but you shouldn't muddle them together. It is linguistically inconsistent to postulate a lonely self as the receiving centre of the data. Therefore, solipsism is a vice of style and not a plight of man.

Nevertheless, as scientific empiricism gained prestige in the nineteenth century, so the undercurrent of solipsistic fear grew, and a number of philosophers gave varied expression to it. Nietzsche's works, for example, contain solipsistic epigrams which, like this one, sometimes anticipate

Conrad's: 'Beliefs are illusions of which we have forgotten that they are illusions.' Schopenhauer, too, a philosopher studied by Conrad, modulates towards solipsism when he emphasizes 'the frailty, vanity and dream-like quality of all things'.[74] Conrad's letters frequently express contradictory paradigms: sometimes (as we have seen) he talks of the universe as a hard, remorseless machine – the deterministic paradigm; yet he can also talk of the individual as a solitary consciousness amid mirage-like flux – the solipsistic paradigm.

The machine is thinner than air and as evanescent as a flash of lightning . . . . . [T]he ardour for reform, improvement for virtue, for knowledge, and even for beauty is only a vain sticking up for appearances as though one were anxious about the cut of one's clothes in a community of blind men. Life knows us not and we do not know life – we don't even know our own thoughts . . . . . Faith is a myth and beliefs shift like mists on a shore.[75]

The sense of extreme subjectivity has numerous consequences in Conrad's works. There are direct expressions: Marlow in 'Heart of Darkness' says 'We live, as we dream – alone', and Conrad liked to quote Calderón's phrase '*La vida es sueño*' ('Life is a dream'), which is recalled by Decoud's thought: '[A]ll this is life, must be life, since it is so much like a dream.'[76] Conradian narrators (including the narrator of *Nostromo*) have the cynical habit of applying the term 'illusions' to ideals, thoughts, observations and feelings – even love is termed merely 'the strongest of illusions'. Another consequence is suggested by A. D. Nuttall's book, *A Common Sky*. Nuttall argues that there 'If a man feels the real world slipping from him, he tightens his grip upon it': the modern taste for vivid concreteness in literature may, in part, be compensatory.[77] Fear that the solipsist case may be valid may generate a demand for reassurance that the world has tangibly solid objectivity. Conrad's works provide an excellent illustration of this thesis. In *Nostromo* there is a grand paradox of texture: the explicit solipsistic comments are supported by descriptive passages which strongly emphasize a dreamlike, phantasmagoric quality of experience; yet innumerable passages emphasize the tangible solidity of our environment. Thus, the remarkably varied textural richnesses of *Nostromo* may stem partly from Conrad's paradoxical imaginative grasp of both determinism and solipsism.

Over the centuries, a familiar half-brother of solipsism has been linguistic subjectivism: the belief that the relationship between language and external reality is illusory or vastly inadequate. A letter from Conrad to Cunninghame Graham expresses this view succinctly:

Half the words we use have no meaning whatever and of the other half each man understands each word after the fashion of his own folly and conceit.[78]

Conrad might have been encouraged in such scepticism by some of the opinions of Maupassant or Anatole France, or by reading Nietzsche or Schopenhauer. Schopenhauer, in turn, derived his views partly from Buddhism. Linguistic subjectivism has a venerable ancestry and has been revived from time to time in the twentieth century: for instance, by existentialism, structuralism and deconstructionism. Their proponents (notably Sartre, Barthes and Derrida) have sometimes made a philosophical melodrama of their disappointment that words are neither equivalent to nor necessarily connected with objects, as if they had expected the word 'bread' to satisfy hunger or to appear automatically on every loaf. There is an entertainingly paradoxical or self-defeating element in their sceptical theories, since the claim that language has only an illusory grasp on reality must itself be made in language; so, if the claim is true, it must be false.

Linguistic scepticism may take hard or soft forms. The hard form denies language any purchase on reality at all (in which case, the proponent would be wasting his time in attempting to communicate such a denial). The soft form stresses not the impossibility of communication but its inadequacy, and its proponent likes to dwell (in words) on the power of words to deceive, delude and offer a false sense of our rational grasp of our environment. In his writings, Conrad flirts occasionally with the hard form but enjoys a more faithful relationship with the soft form. Marlow, in 'Heart of Darkness', declares:

'No, it is impossible; it is impossible to convey the life-sensation of any given epoch of one's existence – that which makes its truth . . . . .'

While, in *Lord Jim*, Marlow adds:

For a moment I had a view of a world that seemed to wear a vast and dismal aspect of disorder . . . . . I went back into my shell directly . . . . . though I seemed to have lost all my words in the chaos of dark thoughts I had contemplated for a second or two beyond the pale. These came back, too, very soon, for words also belong to the sheltering conception of light and order which is our refuge.[79]

A second grand paradox of Conrad's fiction, then, is that in eloquent words he offers warnings against eloquent words; he offers in masterly language the truth that language can falsify and delude. Repeatedly, in *Nostromo*, he depicts the ironic contrast between noble rhetoric and base actuality, between fine professions and ignoble emotions, between creed and deed. All the ardent articulacy of men is mocked at two extremes: at one extreme, by that parrot which cries 'Viva Costaguana', and at the other, by the vast silence of the Placid Gulf and the enduring serenity of Mount Higuerota.

3.8 Music

When, in a letter to William Blackwood, Conrad defined his artistic allegiances, he said that he compared himself not with Scott, Thackeray or George Eliot but with Wagner, Rodin and Whistler:

I am *modern*, and I would rather recall Wagner the musician and Rodin the Sculptor who both had to starve a little in their day – and Whistler the painter who made Ruskin the critic foam at the mouth with scorn and indignation. They too have arrived. They had to suffer for being 'new'.[80]

Almayer's Folly indicates his familiarity with Wagner's *Tristan und Isolde* (1865), and *Nostromo* has some analogies with *Der Ring des Nibelungen* (completed in 1876). It may not be merely coincidental that Conrad's epic novel, like Wagner's opera-cycle, amplifies the ancient legendary thesis that treasure confers both power and a curse, causing dissension and treachery while blighting love. To coordinate his cycle, Wagner elaborated the use of recurrent musical chords, themes and *Leitmotiven* (associatively mnemonic phrases); Conrad provides linguistic equivalents to these devices. Appropriately, the novel's engineer-in-chief perceives orchestral qualities in the scenic vista of the mountain-range, and the narrator remarks of his employer:

Sir John arrived too late to hear the magnificent and inaudible strain sung by the sunset amongst the high peaks of the Sierra.[81]

Part 4 Contents of *Nostromo*

4.1 The Text

4.1.1 THE SERIAL *versus* THE BOOK

Nostromo was first published as a serial in *T.P.'s Weekly* between 29
January and 7 October 1904. It then appeared as a book, published in
London by Harper & Brothers, on 14 October in the same year.

There are thousands of differences between the serial and the book.
Many are petty, but many are substantial and extensive. Some are the
result of house-editing at the publishing houses; some were introduced
by the printers; and others are clearly the work of Conrad himself. The
most obvious difference is that, for the book version, Conrad greatly
expanded the final sequence describing Nostromo's love-relationship
with Giselle Viola; and it is generally the case that Conrad seized many
opportunities to expand the material of Part III, which had been curtailed
partly by pressure of time on the author and partly by editorial excisions
at the magazine's office. Since the book version represents Conrad's
'second thoughts', one might expect the book to be consistently superior;
but this is not so. The direct rendering of Nostromo's courtship of
Giselle, in which the descriptions and dialogue have a derivative, 'maga-
zinish' quality, appears (ironically) not in the magazine but in the book.
In the first third of the novel, on the other hand, the serial text is often
longer; and, in some passages, the serial contains excellent material
which, alas, has not survived in any of the subsequent book texts.
Indeed, a few of the omitted passages clarify what, in the extant versions,
is relatively obscure. A possible explanation is that, in order to com-
pensate for his expansions of the ending of the novel, Conrad made
hasty (and sometimes ill-considered) cuts in the earlier parts.

T.P.'s Weekly, III, p. 270, has a long passage which enriches the
description of the Occidental Province and its problems. Mrs Gould,
travelling the region, is troubled by the scale of poverty: she sees 'the
ragged poor sleeping in the shade', 'the beggars on the steps of the
churches besieging the doors of the house of God', 'old hags, ragged
men, women with hopeless faces, and thin, naked children':

Was the remedy for that, too, in the development of material interests? Charles seemed to hug that belief in his taciturn and observing reserve. He was looking for workmen, and that was proof enough of his theory.

The passage not only adds to the fullness of the social panorama of the region; it also helps to counterbalance the novel's concluding emphasis on the oppressiveness of 'material interests' by making clear that, among other achievements, the mine has solved a massive problem of unemployment and poverty in Sulaco.

Another regrettable omission from the book is a sequence (III, pp. 370–71) dealing with 'the proclamation of the so-called Mandate law of Don Vincente's Dictatorship'. It emphasizes that Ribiera's policies have been hatched by Avellanos and Gould, and it clarifies the nature of the dictatorship:

The Señor Administrador of the Gould concession was pleased with the wording of the Five-year Mandate, which suspended the fundamental laws of the estate, but at the same time aimed at keeping private ambitions from interfering in the work of economic reconstruction. Peace at home and credit abroad! Nothing could be more sane. This was not politics; it was the common-sense watchword of material interests which, once established, would safeguard the honest working of these political institutions which, sound in themselves, had been the shield of plundering demagogues. For it is the fate of institutions to be ever at the mercy of men . . . . .

By making clear that the Ribiera regime 'suspended the fundamental laws' of Costaguana, this account accentuates the irony that Gould's quest to secure the mine and thereby inaugurate an era of law, order and progress has involved him in an intrigue to establish yet another dictatorship. The phrase 'This was not politics' is an instance of implicitly reported thought: Gould may rationalize his manipulations as simple 'common sense' only, but the passage ironically emphasizes the amply political extent of his involvement.

An instance of the way in which Conrad's cutting of the text has introduced an obscurity occurs in the dialogue between Hirsch and Gould. The book (p. 170) offers this:

'It is a great, great foolishness, Don Carlos, all this. The price of hides in Hamburg is gone up – up. Of course the Ribierist Government will do away with all that – when it gets established firmly. Meantime –'
    He sighed.
    'Yes, meantime,' repeated Charles Gould inscrutably.

What is obscure here is the transition from 'The price of hides in

Hamburg is gone up' to 'Of course the Ribierist Government will do away with all that', since the reader will be unable to see how the Ribiera regime can possibly 'do away with' a situation which seems to be European and which should, in any case, delight a hide-merchant like Hirsch. The full version in *T.P.'s Weekly* (III, p. 530) provides ample clarification:

'It is a great, great foolishness, Don Carlos, all this. The price of hides in Hamburg is gone up – up.'

The way the Señor Administrador of the Gould Concession bent his gaze upon him would have been enough to make pause a man less profoundly moved; but the adventurous Israelite from Esmeralda continued dolefully:

'And I have just managed to make a confidential arrangement with the Collector of Customs. You are aware, Don Carlos, that no honest man can afford to pay the preposterous export duties in full and continue in business. So I've made a confidential arrangement with the Señor Collector, a most amiable man, and it is the usual thing in this country,' Hirsh [*sic*] murmured, grasping deferentially Charles's extended hand. 'You know that as well as I do, Don Carlos. Of course, the Ribierist government will do away with all that – when it gets firm – firm. Meantime –'

'Yes, meantime?' interrupted Charles Gould, inscrutably.

The serial version makes full sense: what Ribiera's government is expected to 'do away with' is the widespread corruption, of which the required bribery of the Customs official is so characteristic an example. The book version is obscure because a cut has been clumsily and illogically effected.

Even in matters of punctuation, the book is sometimes inferior to the serial. The punctuation in the book text is usually heavier and fuller; but although this often serves to clarify the sentence structure (by marking off subordinate clauses, for instance), there is at times a loss in fluency, occasional errors are introduced, and sometimes the tone is coarsened. Dr Monygham's account of Teresa Viola's death is punctuated as follows in the serial (IV, p. 70):

The soldier, no less startled, up with his rifle and pulled the trigger, deafening and singeing the engineer, but in his flurry missing him completely. But, look what happens! At the noise of the report the sleeping woman sat up, as if moved by a spring, with a shriek, 'The children, Gian' Battista! Save the children.' I have it in my ears now. It was the truest cry of distress I ever heard. I stood as if paralysed, but the old husband ran across to the bedside stretching out his hands. She clung to them. I could see her eyes go glazed; the old fellow lowered her down on the pillows and then looked at me. She was dead.

The version in the book is considerably more exclamatory: 'Save the children.' becomes 'Save the children!'; 'She clung to them.' becomes 'She clung to them!'; and 'She was dead.' becomes 'She was dead!' The effect is to make the description seem more melodramatic and less restrained.

Sometimes the serial provides a uniquely correct reading of a phrase which in the book (and all subsequent editions) is erroneous. Thus, when the silver-boat is progressing through the night in the Gulf, the darkness lightens, and 'the sail came out of the night like a square block of dense shadow' (III, p. 721). Conrad clearly intended the sail to appear relatively dark against the sky, because a little later it is described as 'the square blotch of darkness'. In the book, however, 'block of dense shadow' was erroneously printed as 'block of dense snow' (p. 232), and this error has been perpetuated.

Another instance of the superiority, in some areas, of the serial text is provided by its version of the awakening of Nostromo. In the more familiar texts, this passage is so fine that it has rightly attracted considerable attention from commentators; but the serial version is undoubtedly superior, partly because it contains a sentence which provides a logical bridge between the statement that Nostromo has a 'lost air' and the subsequent description of his confident stretching. Here is the serial text (IV, p. 262):

At last the conflagration of sea and sky lying embraced and asleep in a flaming contact upon the edge of the world, went out. The red sparks in the water vanished together with the stains of blood in the black mantle draping the sombre head of the Placid Gulf; and a fresh puff of breeze rose, rustling heavily the thick growth of bushes on the ruined earthworks of the fort, and died out with a long soughing stir in the branches of crooked dwarf trees growing upon the rock-like creviced face of a bastion. Nostromo woke up from a fourteen hours' sleep, and arose full length from his lair in the long grass. He stood knee deep among the whispering undulations of the green blades with the lost air of a man just born into the world. But quickly the look of recognition came into his eyes. Handsome, robust, and supple, he threw back his head, flung his arms open, and stretched himself with a slow twist of the waist and a leisurely growling yawn of white teeth, as natural and free from evil in the moment of waking as a magnificent and unconscious wild beast. Then, in the suddenly steadied glance fixed upon nothing from under a forced frown, appeared the man.

Among other changes, the book omits the sentence 'But quickly the look of recognition came into his eyes.', resulting in the following transition (p. 347):

He stood knee deep amongst the whispering undulations of the green blades with the lost air of a man just born into the world. Handsome, robust, and supple, he threw back his head, flung his arms open, and stretched himself with a slow twist of the waist and a leisurely growling yawn of white teeth . . . . .

The omission results in an illogically abrupt transition from the state of feeling lost to the state of feeling relaxed and confident.

Certainly, the book text of *Nostromo* is, on the whole, superior to the serial text, as one might expect. The final sequence is, in the book, much fuller and has stronger thematic emphases. Furthermore, the book eliminates many inconsistencies and petty errors. It is nevertheless true that the serial contains much valuable descriptive and narrative material which did not survive in subsequent versions; and, for every ten variants in which the book version is superior, there are perhaps three or four in which *T.P.'s Weekly* is preferable.

Conrad was an inveterate reviser of his works, and he continued to tinker with the text of *Nostromo* during his lifetime. One consequence is that the first book version contains some important material which is not to be seen in standard subsequent editions. Critics, when discussing a Conrad novel, commonly use an edition that is widely available; this makes it easier for their readers to check the critic's citations. Often the editions cited are the Dent Collected Edition (*Nostromo*, 1947), or the Penguin (1963, revised 1983). But the text which the critic then cites will be one which differs in many details from that of the first trade edition; and it was that first trade edition which was widely reviewed at a time when Conrad was anxiously studying (and learning from) the reviews. Therefore some recent critical appraisals may be unhistorical, in that they may be directed to a text which differs in small but significant ways from the one which first made its mark in the world. The following passage appeared in the 1904 book of *Nostromo* (pp. 352–3), and it had a close counterpart in the serial; but it is entirely absent from extant standard editions like Dent's and Penguin's.

In this harbour at the foot of immense mountains that outlined their peaks amongst the kindled swarm of stars; on this smooth, half-wild sheet of black water serene in its loneliness, whose future of crowded prosperity was being settled not so much by the industry as by the fears, necessities and crimes of men short-sighted in good and evil, the two solitary foreign ships had hoisted their riding lights according to rule. But Nostromo gave no second look to the harbour. Those two ships were present enough to his mind. Either would have been a refuge. It would have been no feat for him to swim off to them. One of them was an Italian barque, which had brought a cargo of timber from Puget

Sound for the railway. He knew her men; in his quality of foreman of all the work done in the harbour he had been able to oblige her captain in some small matter relating to the filling of his water tanks. Bronzed, black-whiskered, and stately, with the impressive gravity of a man too powerful to unbend, he had been invited more than once to drink a glass of Italian vermouth in her cabin. It was well known amongst ship-masters trading along the seaboard that as a matter of sound policy the Capataz of the Cargadores in Sulaco should be propitiated by small civilities, which he seemed to expect as his due. For, in truth, being implicitly trusted by Captain Mitchell, he had, as somebody said, the whole harbour in his pocket. For the rest, an excellent fellow, quite straightforward, everybody agreed.

Subsequent editions preserved the next paragraph, which says that Nostromo contemplated escaping from Sulaco and returning to Italy; but they lack this detailed formulation of the plan of escape. What is more curious is the deletion of the important thematic material which begins this quoted paragraph. The statement that the country's future prosperity 'was being settled not so much by the industry as by the fears, necessities and crimes of men short-sighted in good and evil' specifies one of the major historical ironies which the novel copiously illustrates. Furthermore, in the 'Author's Note' which he provided for the 1918 edition by Dent, Conrad cited as a crucial phrase the very words which were no longer to be found in the text. He said that he had envisioned a story of events flowing from the passions 'of men short-sighted in good and evil'.

The number and intricacy of the changes in the text can be indicated by considering the following passage, taken virtually at random, from the end of the first paragraph of the final chapter. It describes Nostromo's obsession with the stolen silver. *T.P.'s Weekly* (IV, p. 455) gives:

Sometimes during a week's stay, or more, he could only manage one visit – no more. He suffered through his fears as much as through his prudence. To do things by stealth humiliated him. And he suffered most from the concentration of his thought upon the treasure as thought becomes concentrated upon a vision of horror and pain. Never did his unblemished reputation appear more vividly as a matter of life and death.

In the 1904 book (p. 444), it appears thus:

Sometimes during a week's stay, or more, he could only manage one visit to the treasure. And that was all. A couple of ingots. He suffered through his fears as much as through his prudence. To do things by stealth humiliated him. And he suffered most from the concentration of his thought upon the treasure; as thought becomes concentrated, his unblemished reputation appear more vividly as a matter of pain and death.

This version eliminates the awkward repetition of 'more', and is initially more specific; but, in the last four lines, omissions have garbled the sense. In the 1947 Dent edition (p. 523), the garbled lines have vanished, so that the passage is as follows:

Sometimes during a week's stay, or more, he could only manage one visit to the treasure. And that was all. A couple of ingots. He suffered through his fears as much as through his prudence. To do things by stealth humiliated him. And he suffered most from the concentration of his thought upon the treasure.

To sum up this section. In whichever edition we read it, *Nostromo* remains a great novel. The value of citing the first edition (warts and all) is that we are then considering the text that the early reviewers had before them; we are looking at the appropriate text for a historical and contextual consideration. There is no single 'perfect' text of *Nostromo*; some of Conrad's later thoughts resulted in improvements, others did not. The intermittent, occasional superiority of details in the *T.P.'s Weekly* version proves this. Like Proteus, *Nostromo* retains its vigorous identity in different manifestations; but, again like Proteus, *Nostromo* has proved capable of various metamorphoses. The text was never fixed and finished; it retained, during Conrad's lifetime, a capacity for variation and modification. Even Conrad's death did not finalize the text, for subsequent editors and printers introduced, from time to time, their minor modifications – corrections to spelling or accentuation, perhaps, or a revision of punctuation. And the work's nature is incessantly modified as the cultural context changes. Passages which might once have seemed movingly romantic may now seem sentimental; paragraphs which once appeared cynical may now seem accurately realistic. Conrad's general view of history, which by the standards of 1904 was highly sceptical, has undoubtedly been vindicated by the follies and barbarities of subsequent historic events.

4.1.2 HUEFFER'S CONTRIBUTION

In his memoirs, Ford Madox Hueffer (by then using the name Ford Madox Ford) claimed that he had contributed to the writing of *Nostromo* 'to make up the weekly instalment' when Conrad was unwell.[1] This claim has provoked some scepticism from commentators, as Ford's recollections are sometimes unreliable, and he was inclined to exaggerate the literary importance of his partnership with Conrad. Nevertheless, there is evidence that he might have contributed some pages to *Nostromo*.

The novels *The Inheritors* and *Romance* proclaimed on their title-pages the joint authorship of Conrad and Hueffer; most of the actual writing was by the latter. Their long tale, 'The Nature of a Crime', originally bore the pseudonym 'Baron Ignatz von Aschendrof' which masked the identities of the two collaborators. *The Mirror of the Sea* was formally accredited to Conrad alone, even though it is now known that much of the material was furnished by Hueffer (who, accordingly, received a share of the payments):[2] hence the disappointingly flatulent, diffuse style of some parts of *The Mirror*, for Hueffer, though fluently facile, was often less graphic and acute than Conrad.

Part of the manuscript of *Nostromo* is in Hueffer's handwriting: about sixteen pages for the opening of Chapter 5 of Part II, and which constitute most of the eleventh instalment of the serial. Some commentators are now inclined to accept Hueffer's claim that here he was no mere amanuensis but a creative contributor to the novel.[3] This instalment contains the long dialogue between Martin Decoud and Antonia Avellanos at the balcony of the Goulds' dining-room; there is much recapitulation of the politics of the region, and, although the love-relationship between Decoud and Antonia burgeons strongly here, the plot, in other respects, 'marks time'. One editor has pointed out that when Conrad revised this material to prepare it for book publication, he deleted over a hundred words, some of which sound like 'Ford at his most facile' (for instance: 'She was with a sort of reasonable ardour, justifying her father really').[4] The cuts, nevertheless, amount to a very small proportion of these pages; and it should be noted that, if Ford Madox Hueffer was here the author, he has generally made a remarkably good job of sustaining the themes, characterization and local atmosphere in a style which blends unobtrusively with Conrad's. Indeed, a distinguished critic has even cited the balcony scene as revealing 'several of the essentials . . . . . of Conrad's method'.[5]

4.1.3 THE EPIGRAPH

The book's epigraph, 'So foul a sky clears not without a storm', is a quotation from Shakespeare's *King John*, IV, ii, 109. The King is addressing a messenger and refers metaphorically to the expression on the latter's face. He means: 'As your expression is so grim, you must have bad news to relate.' The messenger then reports that the French have already invaded John's realm.

In general, only tenuous connections exist between Conrad's novel of South America and Shakespeare's play about the troubled reign of King John of England, though both works are thematically concerned with political instability and treachery. Probably Conrad seized the line opportunistically, deeming it passably apt for a novel about corruption and civil warfare. If, however, we were to ask some of his characters to interpret the metaphors, the quotation's fruitful ambiguity would soon become apparent. To Mitchell, the storm would be the time of strife which resulted in the establishment of the Occidental Republic with Don Juste López as its head of state. To Cardinal-Archbishop Corbelán and Antonia Avellanos, the storm would be that yet to come: the impending warfare which, in their view, will rectify the injustices propagated by the new order. And the Marxist photographer would see a prophecy of the revolutionary overthrow of capitalism. The reign of Gould as 'King of Sulaco' proves as unenviable as that of King John.

4.2 Chronology and Topography

The provision of maps and chronological tables for a fictional Costaguana is mildly absurd but not entirely innocent. The chronologies may be perniciously useful to readers who merely seek a crib to enable them to strip a text to its paraphrasable plot for their notebooks; but they may be more constructively useful for readers who, rightly, have wrestled with the various resistances to facile comprehension offered by the plot, and who seek reassurance that their opponent is in fact a wise mentor. There are a few chronological anomalies, but most of the references in the book cohere satisfactorily. A crucial reference occurs during Gould's meeting with Holroyd in San Francisco, when Holroyd refers to the long war over the Atacama nitrate fields as though it had reached its completion.[6] That war lasted from 1879 to 1884; so this is one of the reasons for giving their meeting the date 1884; which in turn makes 1890 a probable year for the main action of the novel.

Again, to a large extent the topographical references are consistent and permit reliable maps to be drawn. (One of the few anomalies is that the text appears to locate the railhead both 80 and 180 miles from Sulaco.) The maps, too, may be pernicious or constructive, depending on how they are used: as cribs, bad; as challenges and incentives, good. To become seduced by such details is to betray the novel; to ignore such details is to insult it. Above all, the very disparity between the linear clarity of the table or map and the rich profusion of material deployed by the novel may help the reader to define for himself or herself Conrad's methods and purposes.

When constructing the imaginary Costaguana, Conrad drew on writ-

---

ings about many different locations: Mexico, Colombia, Venezuela, Argentina, Paraguay. He remarked to Edmund Gosse that 'Sulaco is a synthetic product' containing bits of Venezuela, Chile, Mexico and the Golfo de Panamá.[7] Colombia has a large town called Santa Marta and a port called Tumaco (which may have suggested Sulaco) – though there is a Sulaco in Honduras. A real Zapiga can be found in Chile, an Esmeraldas in Ecuador, and an Azuera and a Punta Mala in Panama. An equestrian statue of King Carlos IV stood in the Plaza Mayor of Mexico City until Mexico gained its independence. In its geographical location, Costaguana resembles Colombia more than any other major South American republic, for, like Colombia, it has not only a prominent Santa Marta and a spectacular Cordillera (mountain range) but also both an Atlantic and a Pacific seaboard.

The name 'Costaguana' has sometimes been misinterpreted as 'Bird-Lime Coast'. But 'guano' means both 'birds' excrement' and 'palm tree'; and 'Costaguana' should obviously be translated as 'Palm-Tree Coast', for the text specifies the palm groves of the maritime region, and the national flag displays 'two green palm trees in the middle'.[8]

Table A	General Chronology
DATE	EVENT
16th and 17th centuries	Spanish colonialists develop Sulaco, establishing an ecclesiastical court there. Local trade in ox-hides and indigo. Silver-mine worked by slaves.
1821	Charles Gould's grandfather fights for Bolívar in British regiment at Battle of Carabobo.
1830	San Tomé mine reopens after War of Independence.
1832	Holroyd born.
1840	Monygham born.
1842–62	Giorgio Viola serves under Garibaldi, first at Montevideo, later in Italy.
1850–56	Epoch of civil war in Costaguana; federalism; Sulaco resists union.
1855	Charles Gould's Uncle Harry, President of Sulaco, defeated; shot by order of General Bento.
1856	Guzmán Bento inaugurates his own 'perpetual presidency'. Twelve years of peace begin.
1860	Charles Gould born; Martin Decoud born.
1864	Antonia Avellanos born.

1866	Nostromo born. Don José Avellanos and Dr Monygham arrested.
1867–8	Monygham tortured by Father Berón.
1868	Don José Avellanos pardoned; Bento dies; Monygham released. During the turmoil following Bento's death, the mine-workers kill their English masters; the mine is closed.
1868–74	Three governments come and go; the fourth obliges Gould's father to accept ownership of the mine.
1876	Linda Viola born.
1878	Giselle Viola born.
1884	Gould's father dies; Gould marries Emilia, and they travel to Sulaco; on the way, Gould talks to Holroyd at San Francisco.
1885	Holroyd visits Goulds; Goulds tour Sulaco seeking labour; mine is reopened.
1888	Holroyd and Gould finance revolution to install a compliant government. During the warfare, General Montero aids the Blanco (Conservative) Party. May: Don Vincente Ribiera elected 'President-Dictator'. November: Ribiera inaugurates National Central Railway at Sulaco.
1889	April: Montero revolts, abetted by his brother Pedrito. May: Decoud arrives in Sulaco with new rifles for Barrios.
1890–91	War of Separation which establishes the Occidental Province of Costaguana as the independent State of Sulaco. *See Table B.*
1897	Mitchell takes visitor on tour of Sulaco.
1898	Lighthouse built on Great Isabel.
1899	Mitchell returns to England, having appointed Viola lighthouse-keeper.
1900	Class conflict increasing. Prominent Sulacans (Corbelán, Hernández, Antonia Avellanos) plan war of annexation against Costaguana. Goulds return from European tour. Nostromo killed by Viola. Viola dies.

Table B	Chronology of Central Events

DATE	EVENT
1888, May	Ribiera's 'dictatorship' begins.
November	Railway inaugurated at Sulaco.
1889, April	General Montero revolts.
1890, April 21	Battle of Socorro: defeated by General Montero, Ribiera flees with Pedrito Montero in pursuit.
April 27	Nostromo negotiates with Hernández on behalf of Blancos.
April 28	General Barrios and his troops embark for Cayta. Decoud learns of Ribiera's defeat. Hernández offers aid.
April 29	5 a.m.: Silver arrives in Sulaco.
May 1	Rioting erupts. Hernández's aid is accepted.
May 2	4 a.m.: Nostromo meets Decoud at *Porvenir* office and promises that the lightermen will support the Europeans. 6 a.m.–noon: Sulacan authorities shelter at OSN offices. Ribiera rides into the mob and is rescued by Nostromo and railwaymen. Decoud joins defenders of the Amarilla Club. Authorities escape on *Minerva*. Nostromo leads lightermen against mob and reaches Casa Viola. Hernández rides to Los Hatos to receive refugees. 4 p.m.–9 p.m.: Gamacho and Fuentes decide to lead the Monterist mob. Barrios reaches Cayta. López and others plan capitulation to Montero. Decoud proposes the secession of Sulaco from Costaguana. Pedrito Montero reaches railhead. Corbelán sets out to join Hernández.
May 3	*c.* 1 a.m.–6 a.m.: Nostromo brings Decoud to Viola's and goes to fetch doctor for Teresa Viola. *c.* 6 a.m.: Pedrito leaves railhead. *c.* 7 a.m.: General Sotillo seizes ship at Esmeralda. *c.* 8 p.m.: Decoud writes to his sister from Casa Viola. *c.* 9 p.m.: Lighter sets out across Golfo Plácido. Refugees from Sulaco make for Los Hatos woods. *c.* 11.30 p.m.: Sotillo's vessel collides with lighter. 11.50: Sotillo enters Sulaco harbour.
May 4	Before dawn, Nostromo and Decoud bury silver on Great Isabel; Nostromo swims ashore as day breaks. Meanwhile Sotillo holds Mitchell and Monygham, releasing Mitchell at dawn. *c.* 7 a.m.: Don Juste asks Gould to welcome Pedrito. 8 a.m.: Pedrito arrives in Sulaco. *c.* 8.30 a.m.: Pedrito orates on the Plaza. *c.* 10–12: Gamacho orates. *c.* 6 p.m: Pedrito's messenger delivers demand to Pepe at mine. Pepe plans march on town. Gould defies Pedrito. *c.* 6.30: Nostromo awakens. Sotillo kills Hirsch. *c.* 7 p.m.: Nostromo and Monygham meet at Custom House: Monygham proposes the ride to Cayta. (*Continued on p. 66.*)

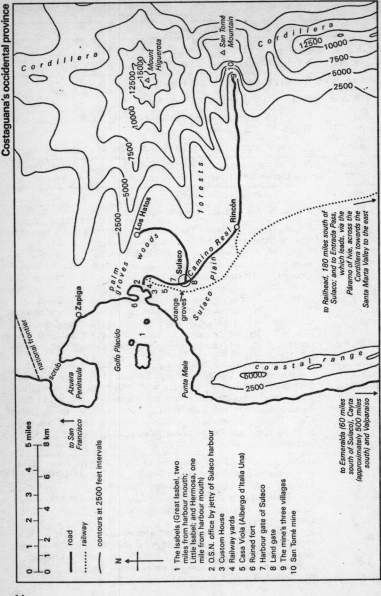

Costaguana's occidental province

Cordillera

△ San Tomé Mountain

Cordillera

△ 15000 Mount Higuerota

12500

12500 10000

7500

5000

2500

10000

7500

5000

2500

f o r e s t s

Rincón

○ Los Hatos

Camino Real

Sulaco

w o o d s

palm groves

orange groves

Sulaco Plain

○ Zapiga

Golfo Placido

Punta Mala

c o a s t a l   r a n g e

5000

2500

national frontier

Scrub

Azuera Peninsula

to San Francisco

to Railhead, 180 miles south of Sulaco; and to Entrada Pass, which leads, via the Páramo of Ivie, across the Cordillera towards the Santa Marta Valley to the east

to Esmeralda (60 miles south of Sulaco), Cayta (approximately 500 miles south) and Valparaiso

N

0	1	2	3	4		5 miles			
0	1	2		4	6		8 km		

road

railway

contours at 2500 feet intervals

1 The Isabels (Great Isabel, two miles from harbour mouth; Little Isabel; and Hermosa, one mile from harbour mouth)
2 O.S.N. office by jetty of Sulaco harbour
3 Custom House
4 Railway yards
5 Casa Viola (Albergo d'Italia Una)
6 Ruined fort
7 Harbour gate of Sulaco
8 Land gate
9 The mine's three villages
10 San Tomé mine

64

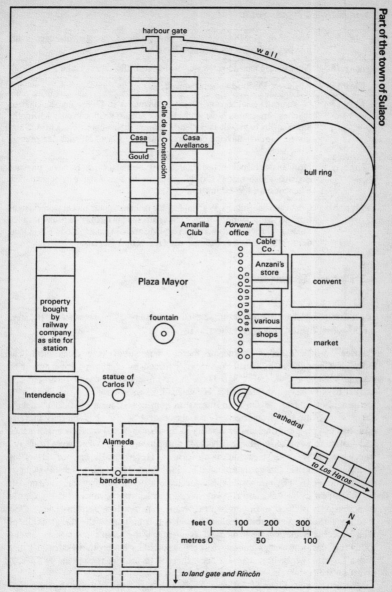

Part of the town of Sulaco

harbour gate

w a l l

Casa Gould

Casa Avellanos

Calle de la Constitución

bull ring

Amarilla Club

Porvenir office

Cable Co.

c o l o n n a d e s

Anzani's store

convent

Plaza Mayor

fountain

various

shops

market

property bought by railway company as site for station

statue of Carlos IV

Intendencia

cathedral

Alameda

to Los Hatos

bandstand

feet 0   100   200   300

metres 0   50   100

N

↓ *to land gate and Rincón*

May 5	Travelling on the engine to the railhead, Nostromo begins his journey to Cayta to summon Barrios.
May 14	At sunset, Decoud rows westward from the Great Isabel.
May 15	At dawn, Decoud shoots himself.
May 17	Nostromo sees Decoud's boat and rows it to Great Isabel. Barrios reaches Sulaco harbour and attacks Sotillo's ship, saving Monygham; Sotillo is killed. Pepe leads miners into Sulaco via Land Gate, saving Gould. Barrios captures Harbour Gate. Hernández presses from west.
June, *c.* 1	Don Juste López promulgates new constitution; Barrios pursues Pedrito southwards; Gould prepares to leave for mission to San Francisco and Washington.
1891, *c.* May	Costaguana–Sulaco War ended by international naval demonstration in Sulaco harbour: US cruiser *Powhattan* salutes flag of Sulaco. General (now Emperor) Montero assassinated. The Occidental Province has become the Occidental Republiç.

4.3 Plot and Techniques

4.3.1 INITIAL SURVEY

If I were obliged to offer a concise plot-summary of *Nostromo* (with, say, a 600-word limit), this might be the result:

Charles Gould's father, a prosperous merchant in Sulaco (the 'Occidental Province' of Costaguana in South America) is forced by a corrupt government to become owner of the derelict San Tomé silver-mine so that the government can extract royalty payments from him. He warns his son to have nothing to do with the mine; but Charles develops an interest in mining and, after his father's death, seeks to renovate the concession. He believes that if he succeeds, he may thereby establish not only commercial prosperity in the region but also a new era of peace and justice to supersede all the turbulent and bloody years of misrule and civil war which have made Costaguana notorious. He is loyally supported by his young wife, Emilia, and gains financial backing from Holroyd, a wealthy American businessman. The renovated mine produces a rich flow of silver; traders visit Sulaco; a new railway is planned. But, in order to secure the mine's future, Gould is increasingly obliged to intervene in Costaguanan politics; with his friend Don José Avellanos, a venerable idealist, he helps to inaugurate the dictatorship of Don Vincente Ribiera, who is pledged to safeguard the 'material interests'. In the following year, however, General Montero, abetted by his brother Pedrito ('Little Pedro'), heads a rebellion; Ribiera flees; there is turmoil in the streets of Sulaco, and for a while the rebels take control there.

Martin Decoud, lover of Antonia Avellanos, conceives the idea that the province of Sulaco should secede from the rest of Costaguana and become an independent republic. During the turmoil, Decoud and Nostromo (famed for his reliability and resourcefulness) take a lighter – an open cargo-boat – into the Placid Gulf in the hope that its cargo of silver can be transferred to a ship and thus to Holroyd. The lighter collides in darkness with a troop-ship commanded by a rebel, Colonel Sotillo, and has to be beached on an island; there Nostromo and Decoud hide the silver, and Nostromo returns to the mainland. Decoud, oppressed by isolation, eventually commits suicide.

General Sotillo hopes to gain the lighter's cargo for himself, but searches unavailingly for it, encouraged in his hopes by Dr Monygham (who thereby plays for time). Pedrito Montero, eager to take control of the San Tomé mine, is warned by Gould that the mine will be blown up if any attempt is made to seize it. Meanwhile, Nostromo has perilously travelled south to bring back to Sulaco the loyal General Barrios and his troops. They engage and defeat Sotillo's forces, while Pedrito Montero's supporters are vanquished by a motley army of mine-workers and former bandits. The Occidental Province secures its independence as a republic, and in the ensuing years its prosperity burgeons. Signs of future turmoil appear, however: prominent citizens argue that Sulaco should now seek to annex the rest of Costaguana, and 'the new cry of wealth for the people' is heard.

Nostromo, meanwhile, has become rich by stealing bars of silver from the hoard on the island; and, though betrothed to Linda Viola, he becomes infatuated by her younger sister, Giselle. The girls' father, Giorgio Viola, is now the keeper of a newly built lighthouse near the hidden treasure. While surreptitiously visiting the hoard, Nostromo is shot by Giorgio, who has mistaken him for an unwanted suitor. Dying, he confesses his theft to Mrs Gould, but she guards his secret; for her, wealth has proved a bitter blessing, as Charles Gould has become increasingly devoted to the mine rather than to her. She has, however, gained the affectionate loyalty of Dr Monygham, who shares her pessimistic vision of a future dominated by 'material interests'.

That's one way of doing it. If you look up Margaret Drabble's summary in *The Oxford Companion to English Literature* you'll see another version.[9] Very different. Hers says less about the politics and more about the personal relationships. A summary reflects the summarizer's preoccupations; that's normal. The most interesting part of the summarizing exercise is probably the mental discomfort it occasions: the sense of going against the grain, or of picking some bones out of a living body.

You'll have noticed that although virtually every critical discussion of *Nostromo* (however sophisticated) entails reference to its plot, a plot-summary of any literary text is practically useless as an indicator of merit. Its usefulness is largely that of contrast: it throws into relief all the features to which a synopsis cannot do justice. In the case of *Nostromo*, it seems to pervert the very originality of the text, since Conrad is concerned to disrupt conventional plotting in order to distribute the reader's attention over a variety of themes, ironies and problems; indeed, he is there concerned to question the very notion of 'plot', whether in fiction or in reality, whether in stories or in histories. He questions it by indicating disparities between the actual nature of life and the stories people tell about life. Conrad hinted at this when he remarked of his novel: 'The historical part is an achievement in mosaic too, though, personally, it seems to me much more true than any history I ever learned.'[10] He perhaps recalled Aristotle's dictum in *Poetics*: '[P]oetry is something more philosophical and more worthy of serious attention than history; for while poetry is concerned with universal truths, history treats of particular facts';[11] but Conrad, aspiring towards paradox, both suggests and subverts the possibility of 'universal truths'. A recent historian, Professor J. F. C. Harrison, has remarked: '[W]e have to remind ourselves continually of the unreality of that peculiar construct, history.'[12] Harrison could almost be stating one of the major themes of *Nostromo*.

Meanings are implicit in techniques, so any summary of the novel which (like that offered a couple of pages ago, or Drabble's in the *Oxford Companion*) ignores the distinctive modes of embodiment of the novel's elements is a falsification of the experienced meanings of the text. When we first begin to read *Nostromo*, one of our strongest impressions is likely to be a bewildering mobility – a kaleidoscopic quality accompanied by an extremity of irony and by a conceptual jaggedness. There are constant shifts in perspective: we're shifted from person to person, from area to area, from one time to another; there's a bright vividness and knobbly concreteness of description, yet also a commentary of aloofly sceptical generalizations. At one minute we're down in the thick of a crowd, being jostled against Nostromo's silver saddle-gear, and at the next we're taking a bird's-eye view of events and places, looking far along the coast and out across the Golfo Plácido. There's an epic scope and a solipsistic undertow. What is prominent in one section dissolves and fades in the next, yet later returns unexpectedly with new prominence. The wheels of the carts aren't simply wooden: they're of thick wood marked with 'the strokes of the axe' – as solid as that; yet, during the night in the Placid Gulf, the world and the self seem about to dissolve into mere blackness. So if, at first reading, you find *Nostromo* bewildering, you're in good company (with V. S. Naipaul),[13] and you may be more attuned to Conrad's questioning intentions than is a less bewildered reader. It's the kind of text that needs to be read at least twice, because many of its ironies can only be appreciated at a second reading; and the novel is concerned repeatedly to question 'readings', whether of history or of individuals. It embodies questions about the very activity of making sense of life. Tolstoy's *War and Peace* has comparable scale and scope, a similar desire to relate great to small, public to private and general to particular; but its exposition is relatively smooth and steady, whereas *Nostromo* is jumpy, pouncy, twisting, erratic, and more starkly radical. *Nostromo*'s techniques lure us into ambushes and set us complex problems of decipherment.

When we have survived those ambushes and look back on the novel, the main pattern of Costaguana's history emerges clearly enough; and the pattern has some distinctive similarities to that detected in (or imposed on) history by Marxists. From the start of his literary career, in *Almayer's Folly* and *An Outcast of the Islands*, Conrad had taken a largely sceptical view of human activities: he had distrusted idealistic and pious rhetoric and had been prompt to suggest the power of economic self-interest operating behind a smoke-screen of noble talk; but it is notable that after the commencement, in 1897, of Conrad's friendship with R. B. Cunninghame Graham (whom Friedrich Engels had described as 'Communist, Marxian, advocating the nationalization of all means of production')[14] a new incisiveness enters his political thought.

In *Nostromo*, numerous aspects of the plot bring Marxism to mind. First, there is the recurrent emphasis on economics as a key to history, the quest for material gain providing the main structure beneath the cultural superstructure of society. ('Your very ideas', wrote Marx and Engels, 'are but the outgrowth of the conditions of your bourgeois production.')[15] Secondly, there is the related suggestion that even if men are not the puppets of a method of production, in the long run the success of men's schemes depends on the compatibility of those schemes with global economic forces. For example: Decoud conceives the idea that Sulaco should secede from Costaguana to become an independent republic; and his scheme comes to fulfilment: an individual's imagination seems to have changed history. But the scheme succeeds because (among other reasons) there occurs a show of force by the United States: we are told that the US warship *Powhattan* was the first to salute the flag of new Sulaco; and the reason for the North American show of force is that a lot of North American capital is invested in the Sulaco silver-mine.

A third feature of *Nostromo* which brings Marxism to mind is the book's emphasis on the ways in which a state's political apparatus can be manipulated in the interests of the wealthy. The best example is provided by Charles Gould's increasing power. Initially, when he plans to redevelop the mine, he says:

'What is wanted here is law, good faith, order, security. Any one can declaim about these things, but I pin my faith to material interests. Only let the material interests once get a firm footing, and they are bound to impose the conditions on which alone they can continue to exist. That's how your money-making is justified here in the face of lawlessness and disorder. It is justified because the security which it demands must be shared with an oppressed people. A better justice will come afterwards. That's your ray of hope.'[16]

However, in order to get the mine established, Gould has to resort to bribery on such a large scale that it soon looks as though a cheaper option will be to finance a coup which will bring to power a so-called dictator, Ribiera, who is pledged to serve the cause of the mine and of foreign investors generally. Conrad clearly relishes the irony that this 'dictator' is the puppet of international capitalism. Nevertheless, the instalment of Ribiera engenders a further coup: the Montero brothers, seeking wealth and power for themselves, are able to exploit nationalist feeling against the foreign investors, racial hostility against the whites and class animosity against the aristocratic land-owning class. Ribiera is overthrown, and Pedro Montero invades the rich western province. For a while the fate of Sulaco hangs in the balance, but eventually the Monterist army is repulsed, and the new state seems to prosper. Nevertheless, near the end of the novel, bitter reflections on Gould's initial hopes for a new era of justice are cast by two of the most astute commentators on events. Dr Monygham says:

'There is no peace and [no] rest in the development of material interests. They have their law and their justice. But it is founded on expediency, and is inhuman; it is without rectitude, without the continuity and the force that can be found only in a moral principle. Mrs. Gould, the time approaches when all that the Gould Concession stands for shall weigh as heavily upon the people as the barbarism, cruelty, and misrule of a few years back.'

And Mrs Gould endorses this view:

She saw the San Tomé mountain hanging over the Campo[,] over the whole land, feared, hated, wealthy, more soulless than any tyrant, more pitiless and autocratic than the worst Government, ready to crush innumerable lives in the expansion of its greatness.[17]

The rhetoric here is not far removed from that of the *Communist Manifesto*:

The bourgeoisie, wherever it has got the upper hand, has put an end to all feudal, patriarchal, idyllic relations. It has pitilessly torn asunder the motley feudal ties that bound man to his 'natural superiors,' and has left remaining no other nexus between man and man than naked self-interest, than callous 'cash payment.'[18]

Now it is certainly true that against the pessimistic outlooks of Monygham and Mrs Gould we have to set, among other things, the optimism of Captain Mitchell. He looks with complacent pride on new Sulaco, with its tramways, department stores and clubs; and (in his view) an era of poverty and civil war seems finally to have been superseded by a tranquil era in which, under parliamentary government, property-owners like himself can look forward to a peaceful retirement enhanced by the income from their shares in the mine, while the masses can enjoy security and a steadily improving standard of living. However, we have been given numerous indications that Mitchell's inner stability and composure depend on a certain thickness of skull; he is honest, generous and reliable, but fails to see the inner pattern of events. Near the end of the novel, the political situation in Sulaco is ominous. The mine-workers have reached a point of class-consciousness; we are told that they are not likely ever again to take up arms to defend the owners. A Communist Party has emerged, and the workers are being urged to rise against the capitalist exploiters. There are predictions of warfare on two fronts. Antonia Avellanos, Cardinal-Archbishop Corbelán and the political refugees from inland Costaguana are plotting a further revolution which would annex Costaguana to Sulaco; and meanwhile Hernández, Minister of War, the ex-bandit who had once supported Gould, has offered himself as military leader to the agitators who hope to 'raise the country with the new cry of wealth for the people'.

So far, so Marxist: apparently an exemplary demonstration of the way in which capitalism, emerging from feudalism, re-shapes in its own interests the political institutions of a country, thrives and prospers for a while, but eventually, through the tendency to monopoly and the creation of a vast and discontented work-force, reaches the phase of internal contradictions which ensures its own downfall. But, of course, the novel offers certain complications.

The most obvious complication is provided by the very pejorative presentation of the Marxist agitator who sits by the bedside of the dying Nostromo. This agitator is 'pale . . . . . , small, frail, bloodthirsty'. He asks Nostromo to bequeath his wealth to the cause, saying 'Do not forget that we want money for our work. The rich must be fought with their own weapons.' This may seem an eminently practical request; more practical than offering pious prayers for a change of hearts, for an increase in benevolence and brotherly feeling. Yet the silver had been regarded as a weapon by Gould, too; and he had discovered that it was a double-edged weapon, 'dangerous to the wielder'. Who guards the guardian? The novel has offered numerous examples of men's judgements being corrupted by the possession of the silver, or by the prospect of possessing it; and all too often the material means to some imagined good has perverted the end or become an end in itself: Gould had reached the point of preferring to be blown sky-high with his mine rather than let the wealth fall into anyone else's hands. One of the factors which makes the weapon of wealth two-edged and dangerous is the short-sightedness of the wielder. The Marxist may well be more short-sighted than Gould, for while sitting at Nostromo's bedside he says: 'You have refused all aid from that doctor. Is he really a dangerous enemy of the people?' Among the causes of Nostromo's refusal of aid from Monygham is guilt: the doctor suspects that Nostromo has stolen the silver, and Nostromo senses the suspicion. An obvious irony implicit in the Marxist's question is the possibility that Dr Monygham, who in the past had suffered hideous torture at the bidding of a dictator, may in the future suffer again, at the hands of one who proclaims the liberation of the oppressed. Another and more general implication is that the old story of the manipulation and exploitation of the many by the few may extend a long time into the future: there may be changes of slogans and changes of masters, but the rapacity, the bloodshed and the parasitism will continue.

During the many years that have elapsed since the publication of *Nostromo*, numerous regimes purporting to be communist have gained power in different parts of the world; and, in the main, those regimes have proved to be élitist, exploitative and tyrannical. Conrad's depiction of the zealous party-member at Nostromo's bedside is strongly caricatural; indeed, in his hunched, attentive and 'bloodthirsty' appearance, the photographer may be intended to recall the vulture which had once settled hopefully beside the slumbering Nostromo after his swim ashore – 'this patient watcher for the signs of death and corruption' – and which, like the photographer, was to be disappointed. Conrad might well feel that his pejorative portrait of the character was vindicated by subsequent history. In 1920, commenting on the Russian Revolution, he said:

These people are unable to see that all they can effect is merely a change of names. The oppressors and the oppressed are all Russians together; and the world is brought once more face to face with the saying that the tiger cannot change his stripes nor the leopard his spots.[19]

4.3.2 THE MEANINGS OF THE TECHNIQUES

Appropriate headings for an examination of the techniques of *Nostromo* are 'transformation', 'defamiliarization', 'delayed decoding' and 'mobility of viewpoint'.

1. *Transformation*

Michael Riffaterre, in *The Semiotics of Poetry*, suggests that the total significance of a poem includes 'the praxis [activity] of the transformation',[20] which is the way in which the poem makes us respond as purposeful transformers of the text before us, so that we seek to maximize the unity and intelligibility of the material. What he suggests there about some poems may well apply to the reading of virtually all literary texts. But it seems to apply peculiarly well to *Nostromo*. Conrad's novel is largely *about* the 'praxis of the transformation'. We see the ironic disparities between various characters' interpretations of experience, and we, in turn, are made exceptionally aware (by the novel's devious unfolding) of the process of reading as a process of decipherment, interpretation and coordination.

2. *Defamiliarization*

Shelley said that poetry 'purges from our inward sight the film of familiarity which obscures from us the wonder of our being'; and his idea was developed by the Russian Formalist, Viktor Shklovsky, who argued (in 'Art as Technique', 1917) that habitual perception devalues life: through familiarity, objects lose vividness: 'Habitualization devours works, clothes, furniture, one's wife, and the fear of war.' Art, however, 'exists that one may recover the sensation of life; it exists to make one feel things, to make the stone *stony*'.[21] So the artist is a 'defamiliarizer', exploiting various devices to make things vivid again. One device is use of an unorthodox viewpoint or stance, to create a disparity between what is conventionally supposed to be happening and what is observed to be happening. Shklovsky did not refer to *Nostromo*, but *Nostromo*, by its rapid shifts in viewpoint and dislocations of chronology, is a rich repository of such devices. One technical paradox of the novel arises when we see that it is also concerned to '*re*familiarize' – as when it uses some 'stock types' of characterization or deploys clarificatory character-summaries.

3. *Delayed Decoding*

This term was originally coined by Ian Watt to refer to a characteristic Conradian descriptive device.[22] Many writers other than Conrad have used it, but seldom with such resourcefulness and searching power. Delayed decoding occurs when the author confronts us with an *effect* while delaying or withholding an explanation of its *cause*. The impact of events is thereby accentuated, and they are often given a quality of strangeness or irrationality which may not be totally eliminated by our eventual comprehension of their rationale. It is an essentially ironic technique, for it dramatizes a disparity between the immediate impact of an experience and its subsequent decipherment by the informed intelligence. It also tends to implicate the reader, from time to time, in the misjudgements or bewilderments of some of the fictional observers. In his exploitation of this method, Conrad was anticipating the technical shock-tactics which became a noted feature of literary Modernism.

Partly as a consequence of the various time-shifts, *Nostromo* contains numerous instances of delayed decoding. A good example occurs in Part III, Chapter 8, when Nostromo climbs the stairs of the Custom House and sees the shadow of a still figure above: 'a shapeless, high-shouldered shadow of somebody standing still, with lowered head, out of his line of sight'. He waits, apprehensive; the figure does not move. Eventually, called upstairs by Monygham, he finds that the shadow's stillness has a clear explanation, for the shadow is that of a man who had been tortured on the strappado and then shot dead. He has a further shock on discovering that the man is Hirsch, whom he had last seen on the boat in the Gulf, and who had apparently been drowned. The reader, who already knows that Hirsch has been brought ashore by Sotillo, still shares part of Nostromo's bewilderment, for it is not until the following chapter that the narrator explains how Hirsch came to be tortured and shot.

We see that the process of delayed decoding usually has three stages: first, there is the impact of a puzzling event; next, there is the initial, incorrect decoding; and eventually there is the correct decoding. In *Nostromo*, Conrad applies this technique on a relatively small scale to numerous events: e.g., the delayed discovery of Hirsch on the lighter, the unseen approach of Sotillo's steamer before the collision, Monygham's inference from Nostromo's reappearance that the lighter's cargo of silver has sunk, or Viola's assumption that the nocturnal visitor to the island is not Nostromo but Ramírez; but, in addition, he applies it on a large scale to the interpretation of historical processes by characters. It is made clear to us that the story of Costaguana's development can be decoded in one way by Mitchell, in another by Gould, in yet another by Decoud, and another by Monygham; and, since the initial presentation of events has been so kaleidoscopic, we become unusually self-aware readers of this narrative of a republic's history. Given the plenitude of data and viewpoints, and given Conrad's inveterate tendency towards paradox, it is not surprising that the various 'delayed decodings' of the text by its subsequent commentators were to display wide disparities. The novel forewarns us of this by emphasizing that 'readings' are interpretations which reflect the needs, biases and fears of the interpreter. This applies to stories and to histories; indeed, one of the purposes of *Nostromo* is to dramatize very starkly the contrast between the two main meanings of the highly ambiguous noun 'history'. 'History' can mean 'the multiplicity of events which occurred within a period of time'; but it can also mean 'a historian's selective account of events which occurred within a period of time'; and there may be a vast disparity between the two.

4. *Mobility of Viewpoint*
Under this heading could be listed at least four subheadings.

(i) *Temporal mobility.* There are unexpected juxtapositions of events from different times: experiences are thrust at us before we are in a position to assess their significance, and, at the first reading of Part I, we may well be confused about the chronological centre of the narrative. Only a small minority of the pages of Part I are set in the narrative present. Gérard Genette has employed the term '*anachronie*' to denote any difference between the time of a reported event and that of its report.[23] Some differences are 'proleptic': a later time is anticipated; others are 'analeptic': a previous time is recalled. In Part I we may well be confused about which is which. For example, on p. 8, Captain Mitchell recalls, as an event in the past, the escape of President-Dictator Ribiera; but later we are shown the inauguration of the same President-Dictator's regime, and many pages will ensue before we learn precisely how and why he was obliged to flee. Thus, an analepsis within Part I proves to be a prolepsis of Part II. Joseph Warren Beach once called this a 'looping method', though he deemed it a failure in the case of *Nostromo* – 'this well-nigh pathless forest'.[24]

All historical novels tend to have a large cast of characters and a wide range of events. Ian Watt has claimed that by making Part I of the novel largely expository, elaborately setting the scene, Conrad can achieve a remarkable concentration in the later parts:

Conrad's complicated series of analepses in Part First of *Nostromo* are essential to the total narrative structure because they enable him to achieve an intense concentration of effect in the central and consecutive parts of the narrative – a concentration which is very rare in historical novels.[25]

(ii) *Visual mobility.* Sometimes our viewpoint seems to be high above the ground, looking down upon the sea or across to the mountains; sometimes it is in the thick of the crowd; and sometimes it is largely congruent with that of one of the characters. In this passage, human beings seem dwarfed and trivialized by the contrast with the vast natural background:

[T]he movements of the animated scene were like the peripeties of a violent game played upon the plain by dwarves mounted and on foot, yelling with tiny throats, under the mountain that seemed a colossal embodiment of silence.

Yet, a few lines later, human actions loom large in the foreground:

In the square of sunlight falling through the door Signora Teresa, kneeling before the chair, had bowed her head, heavy with a twisted mass of ebony hair streaked with silver, into the palm of her hands.[26]

Clearly, one effect of the novel's rapidity of movement between a remote and an intimately close view of human activities is to enable us to experience a paradox which, in its Pascalian form, Conrad knew well. One part of Pascal's formulation was:

The eternal silence of these infinite spaces fills me with dread.

The other part was:

Man is only a reed, the weakest in nature, but he is a thinking reed. There is no need for the whole universe to take up arms to crush him: a vapour, a drop of water is enough to kill him. But even if the universe were to crush him, man would still be nobler than his slayer, because he knows that he is dying and the advantage the universe has over him. The universe knows none of this.[27]

(iii) *Narratorial mobility.* We experience remarkable mobility between informants. Towards the end of the book, much essential information about events is provided by Captain Mitchell's reminiscences to a visitor, and we have to allow for ways in which the information may be distorted by his personality or falsified by his ignorance of some detail. At another point, we are dependent upon a letter being written by Decoud to his sister; and we have to make similar allowances. It is true that for much of the time we have the guidance of, apparently, an omniscient anonymous narrator whose views we may be tempted to identify as Conrad's; yet, at the opening of Chapter 8 in Part I, this narrator actually identifies himself as a mere character, an anonymous visitor to Costaguana: one of those 'whom business or curiosity took to Sulaco in these years before the advent of the railway'.

As this narrator soon resumes the customary spectral mobility of fictional 'omnisciences' (eavesdropping on solitaries, drifting through skulls), we may wonder why Conrad bothered, albeit briefly, to give him a local habitation and identity. The reason may, in part, be psychological: Conrad, like T. S. Eliot when claiming that the narrator of *The Waste Land* is really Tiresias, needs to don a mask, however transparent, in order to speak most eloquently. In 'Heart of Darkness', many subversive points are made in the course of Marlow's tale; and Conrad, if criticized for such observations, could always say: 'Look again: the opinions are identified as Marlow's; they are not necessarily mine.'

Another aspect of the narratorial mobility is Conrad's use of what in German is termed '*erlebte Rede*' and in French '*style indirect libre*': implicitly reported speech or thought. This occurs when, although the text does not there include quotation marks or the phrases 'he said' or 'she said', 'he thought' or 'she thought', we infer that the novel's impersonal narrator is not offering his own reflections but is reporting the reflections of a character. Often the inference is easy and rapid, as in the following description of Sotillo:

All at once, in the midst of the laugh, he became motionless and silent as if turned to stone. He, too, had a prisoner. A prisoner who must, must know the real truth. He would have to be made to speak.[28]

Here it's easy for us to see that the second and subsequent sentences represent the reported thought of Sotillo; the 'must, must' conveys Sotillo's inner impatience, and our awareness that Hirsch has no knowledge of 'the real truth' about the silver confirms our sense, here, of differentiation between the narrator and the character. Elsewhere, however, implicit reportage is a possibility lacking confirmation, so that the degree of authority of a statement remains unresolved. An important instance occurs in the last paragraph of the novel, after Linda Viola has called out Nostromo's name, Gian' Battista:

Dr Monygham, pulling round in the police galley, heard the name pass over his head. It was another of Nostromo's successes, the greater, the most enviable, the most sinister of all.[29]

There has been a high proportion of implied reportage in Part III of the novel, and a statement such as 'Dr Monygham . . . . . heard the name pass over his head' could well be regarded as a cue for a passage of such reported thought. So the second sentence in the quoted passage might merely report Monygham's reflections; or it might have greater authority as a statement representing the narrator's judgements. The ambiguity may be appropriate, giving the sentence a status which is transitional between the viewpoint of the observed character, Monygham, and the narratorial viewpoint which prevails in the surging rhetoric at the end of this final paragraph:

. . . . . the genius of the magnificent Capataz de Cargadores dominated the dark Gulf containing his conquests of treasure and love.

A tricky aspect of narratorial mobility is illustrated in the following passage, describing Hirsch suffering the strappado:

Sotillo, followed by the soldiers, had left the room. The sentry on the landing presented arms. Hirsch went on screaming all alone behind the half-closed jalousies, while the sunshine, reflected from the water of the harbour, made an ever-running ripple of light high up on the wall. He screamed with uplifted eyebrows and a wide open mouth – incredibly wide, black, enormous, full of teeth – comical.[30]

The disturbing feature of this passage is, of course, the notion that a man suffering hideous agony by torture can be regarded as not merely grotesque but positively comical. The judgement seems to be so callous that we might well hope to delegate it as the implicitly reported thought of some brutal observer. But we are specifically denied such recourse. The text specifies that Hirsch is now 'all alone' in the room. The only 'observer' must be the impersonal narrator, who, after referring to the screams, coolly 'aestheticizes' the scene by noting the incongruously beautiful 'ever-running ripple of light', and then contemplates with a pathologist's interest the 'wide open mouth' before declaring Hirsch's appearance 'comical'. The narrator appears to be distinctly callous; yet the same narrator, in other passages of the book, has made clear his condemnation of man's inhumanity to man, and notably of the inhumanity of torture – particularly the torture (akin to Hirsch's) inflicted on Monygham. Hence my determination, throughout this discussion, to refer to the observing presence as 'the narrator' rather than Conrad. What frequently happens in *Nostromo* is that Conrad deploys various kinds of 'observing presence': he subdivides himself into viewers whose values overlap but vary. In this case, the viewer who is briefly deployed is one who shares with his narratorial kindred a relish for the visually incongruous and absurd, but who (regrettably) has let such relish modulate into a capacity to see the horrific as merely farcical.

(iv) *Analogical mobility:* the postulation of analogies between different characters or entities. We may be considering one character, and an unexpected analogy may oblige us to shift our considerations to another, and thus to establish a comparative judgement. We think we're looking at A, and suddenly we find we're simultaneously looking at B. Again, this is quite a common device (George Eliot was particularly skilled in its use), but *Nostromo* exploits it very fully. The critic Cleanth Brooks once said that in *The Waste Land* we are repeatedly shown apparent similarities which reveal underlying contrasts, and apparent contrasts which reveal underlying similarities.[31] In *Nostromo* this technique interlinks numerous characters and historical phases. For example: Nostromo and Gould, though outwardly so different from each other, are both corrupted by their possession of silver (or in their possession by it); and Dr Monygham's reticent love for Mrs Gould is compared with a secret store of unlawful treasure, so Monygham is thus linked to the Nostromo he distrusts. The emissary from Hernandez, the bandit, asks: 'Has not the master of the mine any message to send to Hernández, the master of the Campo?' – and the phrasing invites us to see not only contrast but also analogies between the two determined leaders, and to reflect on the irony that an advocate of 'law and order' is being pressed into complicity with a brigand. Another instance is that Charles Gould, a proudly equestrian figure, is juxtaposed with another equestrian named Charles – King Carlos IV of Spain, depicted in a work of sculpture as a horse-rider:

[T]he big equestrian statue of Charles IV. at the entrance to the Alameda, towering white against the trees, was only known to the folk from the country and to the beggars of the town that slept on the steps around the pedestal, as the Horse of Stone. The other Carlos, turning off to the left with a rapid clatter of hoofs on the disjointed pavement – Don Carlos Gould in his English clothes, looked as incongruous, but much more at home, than the kingly cavalier reining in his steed on the pedestal above the sleeping leperos, with his marble arm raised towards the heavy rim of a plumed hat.[32]

Critical Studies: Nostromo

The mounted king, we are told, seems 'inscrutable', and the other horseman did not 'wear his heart on the sleeve of his English coat'. Except for some awkward syntax, it's a fine descriptive passage, sharply detailed and rich in subtly ironic suggestions. The contrast between the animate and inanimate is stressed, together with the absurdity of a regal figure frozen in immobility above beggars and *leperos* (outcast wretches). The disparity between human pride and human wretchedness is emphasized, too; while questions are raised about the value of powerful figures whose legacy is an impoverished people, and who, for all their readiness to be 'immortalized' by art, may become so forgotten that it is a horse, and not a king, who eventually provides the name of one such memorial. King Carlos IV was the last of the Spanish emperors of South America; his juxtaposition with Gould makes us reflect that a 'captain of industry' may be his present-day counterpart; and, indeed, Gould becomes known as '*El Rey de Sulaco*' (King of Sulaco). In turn, this leads us to consider whether, for all the appearances of progress, the old story is being repeated – the story of exploiters and exploited, of over-lords and the subjugated, of imperialism whether martial or economic. When Gould's 'reign' is secured, the old statue of King Carlos is removed 'as an anachronism'. A final irony, anticipated by that initial descriptive juxtaposition, is that as Gould succeeds in his schemes, he becomes increasingly 'stony' in nature: emotionally inhibited and temperamentally inflexible; rigid, laconic.

Gould thus illustrates a further analogue: he reminds us of those 'gringos' described at the book's opening, who sought the treasure of Azuera and who, 'spectral and alive, are believed to be dwelling to this day amongst the rocks, under the fatal spell of their success'. This opening is variously proleptic: it anticipates not only Nostromo's fatal attachment to his stolen hoard of silver, but also Gould's enslavement, too, to the wealth of his mine. He may, eventually, be involuntarily liberated from it. King Carlos IV lost his empire when the people rebelled; possibly we are meant to speculate that the new 'King' Carlos may lose *his* empire (the *imperium in imperio*) in the stormy future foreseen by Monygham and Corbelán. Conrad provides some conventional 'closures' at the end of his novel (the deaths of Nostromo and Viola), but, by the range of prophetic and predictive utterances, he also provides some less conventional 'openings' on further vistas, further potential narratives.

4.3.3 CONSIDERATION OF THE TIME-SHIFTS

One of the most influential commentators on *Nostromo*, Jocelyn Baines, offered this theory to account for the time-shifts:

> The elimination of progression from one event to another . . . . . has the effect of implying that nothing is ever achieved. By the end of the book we are virtually back to where we started; it looks as if the future of Costaguana will be very similar to her past.[33]

'[N]othing is ever achieved'. A technical innovation is, according to this theory, convertible into a conservative political recommendation: man should resign himself to the fact that he is incapable of making substantial or enduring improvements in his condition. We can test this interpretation by considering two of the most striking examples of the time-shifts.

In Part I, Chapter 2, Mitchell tells how Dictator Ribiera fled to Sulaco on a lame mule, was nearly assassinated by the mob, but was rescued by Nostromo and eventually departed by sea to safety. In this account, we gain information about the somewhat patronizing character of Mitchell and the remarkably resourceful character of Nostromo, and we may suppose that this information will be useful in the ensuing narrative; but we are also likely to think that the Ribiera incident is past history, outstripped by the unfolding narrative. Yet, in that last respect we have been deceived, for the subsequent narrative spirals gradually back in time, so that about a hundred pages after the account of Ribiera's downfall we are told of the inauguration of his regime. Then the narrative slowly spirals forward in time, so that many pages later, in Part II, Chapter 7, Decoud records as yesterday's occurrence the very event that Mitchell had described near the beginning of the book: 'The missing President, Ribiera, ... has turned up here . . . . . , riding on a lame mule into the very midst of the street fighting.'

Such deviousness in the narrative has various functions. First, this technique gives an unusual plausibility to the fictional historical events. When one character, near the middle of the novel, reports as yesterday's occurrence an incident that a different character, early in the novel, had reported from a different viewpoint and with a different emphasis, the incident acquires a stereoscopic quality. Secondly, the method gives a tentacular quality to the ironies. If normal chronological narration had been used, we would have learned first about Ribiera's pious hopes at his inaugural banquet and much later about his ludicrous escape on the mule, and the latter event would have lent a retrospective irony to the former. But the proleptic narration, by telling us in advance of his flight, makes us thoroughly sceptical spectators of the banquet: its rhetoric now has a hollow ring. Thirdly, as Baines noted, the sense of history as cyclical and repetitive plays against the sense that history displays a steady evolution. As the narrative impinges on us, Ribiera has his downfall, Ribiera is put into power, Ribiera has his downfall: a cycle. As we rearrange the events to make orthodox narrative sense, Ribiera is established by the financial powers in order to safeguard their interests; he is overthrown; and out of the ensuing turmoil a new independent state emerges. In one sense, there is no going back: the modern state cannot be unmade. But in another sense, of which the narrative fluctuations have reminded us, there is a constant recurrence of folly and exploitation, though in varying forms.

Fourthly, and perhaps most importantly, the time-shifts and the related dislocations in the narrative have value as resistances to be overcome: and thus they include what might be termed a moral and political therapy. Conrad said that the book depicted 'the passions of men short-sighted in good and evil'. *Nostromo* provides many examples of such moral myopia. There's Gould, unable to foresee the ways in which the mine may corrupt his judgement; Mitchell, complacent about the social changes and insensitive both to the agonies entailed and to the new strife to come; and Ribiera, failing to foresee the brevity of his regime. There are frequent misjudgements of one character by another; some people sacrifice present life on the altar of an imagined future; others are blinded to the future by the immediately present. Conrad's oblique method could almost have been designed to induce in the reader the very flexibility that most of the main figures in the novel lack, and suffer from lacking. Thus, while demonstrating the political infancy of men, the novel embodies its own political maturity in techniques which entail for the reader an education in that maturity. By delaying the decoding of events, Conrad forces us to share the myopia of his characters; but, by provoking the decoding, he provides a therapy which helps us to share his own keen vision.

Or so one could argue; but this interpretation would certainly be challenged by some other commentators. Albert Guerard, for instance, has claimed that Conrad maliciously frustrates the reader's attempt to grasp the story: 'The novelist . . . . . maliciously chops at his hands'; furthermore, Part III is marred by an 'uncertain or uselessly wavering point of view'.[34] There *are* some signs of authorial haste or flagging energies in the third part of the book; but, against Guerard, it could be argued that the shifts in viewpoint are, demonstrably, still highly functional. The best example of this is provided by the location of the long, vivid and plangently memorable description of Decoud's isolation on the island.

Decoud caught himself entertaining a doubt of his own individuality. It had merged into the world of cloud and water, of natural forces and forms of nature. In our activity alone do we find the sustaining illusion of an independent existence as against the whole scheme of things of which we form a helpless part.

Eventually, oppressed and demoralized by exhaustion and solitude, he shoots himself:

The stiffness of the fingers relaxed, and the lover of Antonia Avellanos rolled overboard without having heard the cord of silence snap aloud in the solitude of the placid gulf, whose glittering surface remained untroubled by the fall of his body.[35]

One reason for the widely acknowledged power of this sequence is that both Decoud's death and the comments on it form a thematic nexus: they sum up majestically in image and epigram some of the strongest thematic implications of the work, and those implications have previously been pressing on us, largely subliminally, in a great variety of ways.

When Decoud beholds the universe as 'a succession of incomprehensible images', the possible validity of this view has been increased by our initial bewilderment by the time-shifts, which have given an impressionistic vividness but also a dislocation to events. Our plight may well have resembled that of the visitor to Costaguana who, on listening to Mitchell's reminiscences, was

stunned and as it were annihilated mentally by a sudden surfeit of sights, sounds, names, facts, and complicated information imperfectly apprehended . . . . .[36]

Eventually, of course, we have sorted the images and given comprehensibility to the initially incomprehensible: the decoding, though often frustrated and delayed, has gradually become less difficult. But that initial sense of confusion has at least invoked the possibility that the world, truly perceived, may be recalcitrant to man's decoding endeavours. Conrad had told Cunninghame Graham: 'Life knows us not and we do not know life – we don't even know our own thoughts.'[37] Another consequence of the complex narrative techniques has been the prominence gained by the few constant features in the imaginative landscape: throughout the temporal changes, for all the shifts of action in the foreground, the scenic background has remained constant: the Placid Gulf itself, the cool and unchanging snow-capped Cordillera, and the vastly serene and icy Mount Higuerota. So, when the glittering surface of the Placid Gulf remains untroubled by the fall of Decoud's body, this comes as a seemingly inevitable illustration of the narrator's maxim about 'the whole scheme of things of which we form a helpless part'.

As for the *political* implications of that maxim about 'the whole scheme of things', they are not necessarily what they first seem to be. The easy reading is to take them as classically conservative: men may come and men may go, but in the long run the Godless non-human environment prevails: in the long run, man is impotent. However, if we remember that *Nostromo* first appeared in 1904 (when the European nations were still wrangling about their acquisitions in Africa and other parts of the globe, and when advocates of imperialism far outnumbered their opponents), one implication is clearly anti-imperialistic, for it associates imperial activity by nations with the action which is only a sustaining 'illusion' in individuals.

If Conrad had followed orthodox chronological order, the death of Decoud would have been described long *before* Mitchell's résumé of the subsequent events. The time-shift method enables Conrad to reverse the orthodox order, so that the death scene follows immediately *after* that long complacent account of the ostensibly progressive evolution of Sulaco. For Mitchell, history has been progressive: the story of Sulaco has a happy ending; man has mastered nature, and civilized man has mastered society. Almost immediately after these reflections, Conrad deploys the most vivid example of human littleness. Scepticism is validated in a scene which shows the self-destruction of the sceptic.

In the essay 'Autocracy and War' (1905), Conrad argued that the governments of states, like individual men, are in moral infancy. Fearing destruction, they react aggressively.

The idea of ceasing to grow in territory, in strength, in wealth, in influence – in anything but wisdom and self-knowledge [–] is odious to them as the omen of an end . . . . . Let us act lest we perish – is the cry.[38]

So there he commends not aggressive action but 'wisdom and self-knowledge': a phrase which, in the essay, may sound suspiciously vague and cloudy. It begs many questions; it needs many examples. But the novel *Nostromo* had answered some of those questions and provided some of the examples. The wisdom that Conrad had commended in the novel, by implication and through irony, had entailed ample indignation on behalf of the humble, the exploited and the cannon-fodder of history. The wisdom had entailed ample scepticism, about political jargon and rhetoric, about the possibility that a just society could ever be found under conditions of economic imperialism. Yet that wisdom had entailed a hope that can be glimpsed in the challenges afforded by the novel's shifts in time and space, with their therapy for short-sightedness: a hope that some people may work towards maturity by developing and increasing the ability to apply to the present the lessons of the past, to have foresight which does not require the sacrifice of the life of the present, and to test all general doctrines by a mobile responsiveness to individual human experience. As Mrs Gould reflects: '[F]or life to be large and full, it must contain the care of the past and of the future in every passing moment of the present.'[39] Of course, she remains a lonely and largely defeated figure. A major source of the ironies of *Nostromo* is Conrad's sense that the values most worth preserving are not those most likely to prevail; but without the sense of those values frustrated (and intermittently rendered absurd by the immensity of the non-human environment), the book would lack its eloquent intensity of pessimistic realism.

When the techniques of *Nostromo* have opened our eyes, we may look on that novel not, finally, as 'a succession of incomprehensible images', but rather as the engineer looked on Mount Higuerota,

thinking that in this sight, as in a piece of inspired music, there could be found together the utmost delicacy of shaded expression and a stupendous magnificence of effect.[40]

4.4 The Interaction of Themes and Characterization

It is typical of the strategies of *Nostromo* that the characterization is conceived in such strongly thematic terms that it is remarkably difficult to discuss one character without discussing several. *Nostromo* is a powerfully psycho-political novel. By 'psycho-political' I mean that Conrad conceives human psychology largely in terms of political history, and political history largely in terms of human psychology. One of the clearest instances is provided by Gould's increasing infatuation with the mine, an infatuation which has its idealistic political rationale, but which leads him into a form of infidelity to his wife: eventually he sleeps at the mine, with the mine, rather than with Emilia, and she becomes stoically resigned to childlessness. An explicit theme of the novel is the tendency of men to form 'an ideal conception' which then may become a kind of monomania, whether it be a political ideal or a self-image.

One grouping of characters is that of Decoud, Monygham and (eventually) Emilia Gould: they are sceptical observers of 'material interests'. Another grouping is that of characters who are fatally attracted by treasure: Charles Gould, Nostromo, Sotillo and the gringos of the Azuera. Gould is also linked with Nostromo and Decoud, for all three have defied the advice of their elders. Gould reopens the mine in defiance of his father's warning; Nostromo goes to sea with the silver in defiance of Teresa's admonitions and in disregard of her plea for a priest to be fetched; and Decoud's scheme for an independent Sulaco rejects the centralist doctrine of Avellanos's *Fifty Years of Misrule.*

Yet another interconnected group is constituted by Don José Avellanos, Dr Monygham and Señor Hirsch, for all are victims of cruelty. Avellanos has suffered under the tyranny of Guzmán Bento but has nevertheless preserved his political idealism and his hopes for the future. Those hopes, however, are largely mocked by the débâcle of the Ribiera regime; and though, dying, he may appear to bless Decoud's plan for the independence of the Occidental Province, his gesture is the ambiguous response of an exhausted and moribund figure. Monygham has suffered atrociously at the hands of Bento's torturers; having confessed to participation in a non-existent conspiracy, he feels his life is tainted, and, as a dour, embittered figure, is widely disliked and distrusted. He is kindly patronized by Mrs Gould; gradually, he develops a reticent love for her and a private jealousy of her unloving husband. Largely for Emilia Gould's sake, he offers himself as a would-be informer to Sotillo; by falsely keeping alive Sotillo's hopes of finding the silver, he prevents an alliance of Sotillo with Pedrito Montero; and thereby, risking his life, he aids the loyal forces which eventually recapture Sulaco. On the other hand, his responsibility for Nostromo's fall into corruption is greater than he ever realizes: he puts into Nostromo's mind the idea that only the whole cargo of silver could be an adequate reward for his risks; and, when Nostromo has swum ashore, Monygham's lack of concern for the cargo is one of the factors which ensure the Capataz's determination to become his own man rather than the loyal servant of the mine. A particularly cruel irony, as Nostromo points out, is that if Monygham had not chosen to let Sotillo think that the silver was hidden in the bay, Sotillo would not have inflicted upon Hirsch tortures as excruciating, if not as protracted, as those endured by Monygham in the past.

The characterization of Hirsch does seem to be tainted by anti-Semitism. True to an anti-Semitic stereotype, Hirsch, when we first see him, is anxiously eager to make profit by trade, dislikes the region into which the quest for profit has brought him, and is capable of abject cowardice. His agonies of fear during the revolutionary upheavals are treated in a black comic manner, contrasting with the compassionate account of Monygham's former suffering; when found cowering on the lighter, he is regarded with scorn by Nostromo; and even during his torture on the strappado, there occurs a moment when (as we have seen) the impersonal narrator regards his appearance as 'comical'. On the other hand, this harshness of presentation is mitigated by various factors. One is that the circumstances of the torture are so fully presented that pity for Hirsch and contempt for his grotesque torturer are predominant in the reader's mind; and Hirsch, who had previously been so abject, at least makes a desperate defiance of his captor by spitting in his face. (If we recall that this was also Garibaldi's act of defiance when under torture, Hirsch briefly becomes a comrade-in-suffering of the liberator revered by Viola.) Furthermore, since the most explicit expressions of anti-Semitic prejudice ('Speak, thou Jewish child of the devil') are those uttered by the torturer, Sotillo, the text offers its warnings of the brutal concomitants of anti-Semitic prejudice: one of the instances of a politically prophetic quality in the work. As a whole, the characterization of Hirsch may still give the reader the uneasy feeling that Conrad's humanity has not sufficiently resisted the easy option of a prejudicial stereotype.

One of Hirsch's functions in the novel is, of course, to offset (by contrast with his cowardice) the intrepid resourcefulness of Nostromo. As we have noted elsewhere, Nostromo's character is not fully convincing, even though his development is provided with ample motivation, and even though he functions importantly in the thematic range and is a central figure in the plot-sequence which culminates in the establishment of the new state of Sulaco. A difficulty is that there seems to be some disparity between the elaborate analysis of his significance which the narrator provides and the frequently rather melodramatic, certainly theatrical, dialogue which Nostromo utters. ('By all the saints and devils I shall let the sea have the treasure rather than give it up to any stranger ..... [M]ay the curse of heaven fall upon this blind gulf! ..... Caramba!') We are reminded that Conrad's works often incorporate, though they usually sophisticate, some elements of popular adventure-novels. Stylistically, the nadir of the novel is probably reached during

Nostromo's illicit courtship of Giselle: there, both the dialogue and the narratorial commentary seem to derive from second-rate romantic fiction:

> He broke out –
>
> 'Your hair like gold, and your eyes like violets, and your lips like the rose; your round arms, your white throat.' . . .
>
> Imperturbable in the indolence of her pose, she blushed deeply all over to the roots of her hair. She was not conceited. She was no more self-conscious than a flower. But she was pleased. And perhaps even a flower loves to hear itself praised. He glanced down, and added, impetuously –
>
> 'Your little feet!'[41]

(The line 'perhaps even a flower loves to hear itself praised' confirms the impression that a less intelligent side of Conrad seems to have undertaken the writing at this point.) It is widely recognized by critics that Conrad is seldom at his best when describing passionate sexual encounters. On the other hand, he can be very effective when describing sexual relationships in which there is an element of alienation and inhibition. The presentation of Mrs Gould and the slow decline of her marriage to Charles is one of the clearest instances. It is true that Emilia Gould belongs to a long literary tradition: the tradition of the 'Lady Almoner': the idealistic woman who, though disappointed by life, nevertheless seeks compensation and consolation in her charitable works for others. (Familiar examples of the type include the eponymous heroine of George Eliot's *Romola*, Dorothea in Eliot's *Middlemarch*, and Elizabeth Gaskell's Margaret.) The type is, however, convincingly individuated in *Nostromo*, and Mrs Gould's good endeavours for other people (the establishment of a hospital run by Monygham, her care for Viola and his daughters, and her sympathy with Don José, Decoud and Antonia) can be seen not only as her compensation for emotional disappointment, not only as vicarious fulfilment of frustrated motherhood, but also as a strong political positive in the book. Others may conceive ambitious or idealistic schemes; Mrs Gould does what she can, on a practical and personal basis, to improve locally the lives of individuals. Hers are limited but solid achievements, and her personal involvement with others' lives mitigates the tendency of the economic process to depersonalize relationships.

One commentator, Ugo Mursia, has suggested that an important polarity of the book is the contrast between 'Our Man' (Nostromo) and 'My Lady' (Madonna):[42] Nostromo is egoistic, but Emilia Gould is almost saintly in her altruism; and Emilia is associated by the text with the figure of the Madonna, St Mary, which stands in her house. As Charles is associated with the statue of a king, Emilia is associated with the statue of a saint. She has also, as a study of a sympathetic participant maturing towards stoical composure, elicited some of Conrad's subtlest and most perceptive writing. The scene (in Part I, Chapter 6) in which Charles proposes marriage to her is finely sensitive and unconventional, even to the detail of the dropped parasol bouncing away 'with a martial sound of drum-taps'. In the book's large-scale comparative network, Mrs Gould is clearly linked with Teresa Viola and Antonia Avellanos. Teresa, like Emilia, suffers silently and has paid a heavy price for her marriage to a man with a political obsession: again, there is a sense that the husband's political preoccupation, though retaining an almost heroic value and consistency, has betrayed or impoverished the personal relationship. Antonia, in turn, seems destined to remain childless and unfulfilled because of her devotion to the memory of Martin Decoud, whose love for her was not sufficiently great to withstand his scepticism. It may seem rather stereotypical that in this novel the outstanding instances of selfless devotion are provided by ardent women; but the stereotype has ample warrant in historical reality (famously, in Florence Nightingale and, later, Edith Cavell, for example). Though Conrad's works seldom provide gratification for feminists, Antonia Avellanos does have some features of the 'New Woman' of the late nineteenth century: she is, by local standards, sexually emancipated, highly articulate and politically committed; and the book does, as a whole, cast an unflattering light on the political immaturities of males and on the injustices of a powerfully patriarchal society. A significant detail of this theme is that the main female characters are betrayed or disappointed by the men whom they trust: Nostromo's infidelity to his fiancée, Linda Viola, is merely the most glaring instance.

The political intelligence of the text is suggested by its prophetic features. Though Conrad based his work largely on memoirs of life in South America in the mid nineteenth century, his analysis of the plight and problems of South American republics has held good, to a surprising extent, for that area in the twentieth century. The turbulence has continued; man's inhumanity to man has repeatedly been demonstrated by the tyrannies and repressions in that region; and sometimes a source of tension has been the attempts by North America to extend its influence in the central and southern areas of the continent. In the light of subsequent history, the depiction of Holroyd seems, within its mode of mildly parodic exaggeration, to contain an astute sense of things to come; Holroyd, who in this novel of 1904 says of the United States:

Critical Studies: Nostromo

'Of course, some day we shall step in. We are bound to. But there's no hurry. Time itself has got to wait on the greatest country in the whole of God's Universe. We shall be giving the word for everything; industry, trade, law, journalism, art, politics, and religion, from Cape Horn clear over to Smith's Sound, and beyond, too, if anything worth taking hold of turns up at the North Pole. And then we shall have the leisure to take in hand the outlying islands and continents of the earth. We shall run the world's business whether the world likes it or not. The world can't help it – and neither can we, I guess.'[43]

'The world can't help it – and neither can we . . . . .' The phrasing underlines the historic irony that the strivings of men, if successful, seem paradoxically to be fulfilling a predetermined pattern of economic evolution. Activities which, in the near view, seem to demonstrate human free will and potency, seem from a longer perspective to demonstrate the subjugation of men to a global economic machine. We may recall that, shortly after writing *Nostromo*, Conrad published the essay 'Autocracy and War', with its prophecy of the cataclysm of 1914–18:

Industrialism and commercialism – wearing high-sounding names in many languages (*Welt-politik* may serve for one instance) . . . . . – stand ready, almost eager, to appeal to the sword as soon as the globe of the earth has shrunk beneath our growing numbers by another ell or so. And democracy, which has elected to pin its faith to the supremacy of material interests, will have to fight their battles to the bitter end . . . . .[44]

An American critic eventually remarked of *Nostromo* that 'the novel's own view of history is skeptical and disillusioned, which for us today must mean true'.[45] Conrad had already observed, however, that those who deem themselves to be disillusioned have preserved at least one illusion – namely, that they are disillusioned.

4.5 The Character of the Ubiquitous Narrator

An 'inner narrator' is a character who, for a while, dominates the foreground as a person providing extensive information about events. Near *Nostromo*'s beginning and ending, Mitchell takes this role; near the novel's centre, Decoud (writing to his sister) takes it. One function of such inner reports is to provide insight into the character of the reporter; another is to accelerate the pace of the novel by providing a relatively succinct account of many events which might otherwise take hundreds of pages to unfold. Throughout the novel, of course, we are dependent on the ubiquitous, impersonal 'outer' narrator: it's he who looks over

Decoud's shoulder at the letter; it's he who overhears Mitchell's conversations. We have noted that at the outset of Chapter 8 of Part I, this ubiquitous narrator suddenly identifies himself as a character, a visitor to Sulaco; but that identification (which the author probably found psychologically convenient as a nominal mask) is soon forgotten by most readers, as it is clearly inconsistent with his customary narratorial freedom to roam through time and space, to monitor thoughts and to spy on solitaries.

Although Joseph Conrad is the author of every statement by the ubiquitous narrator, the latter should not be identified as Joseph Conrad. The character of such a narrator will vary according to the nature and implications of the narrative to be unfolded; and, though he is 'impersonal' in the sense of being anonymous and (usually) disembodied, his observations nevertheless imply a personality. An imagined outer narrator may precede, and evoke from the author, a particular narrative; more often, the author deploys the kind of narratorial personality that seems most conveniently and fruitfully adapted to (or elicited by) the potentialities of the envisaged narrative. In *The Secret Agent*, for example, that deployed narrator is generally more coldly sardonic and mocking in tone than his counterpart in *Nostromo*. As *The Secret Agent* is concerned largely with anarchists and their sordid milieu in London, its narrator has a personality of fastidious scorn, sardonic humour and fascinated distaste which is implied by his numerous ironic, satiric and mock-heroic devices and by his coolly analytic responses to violent death. The ubiquitous narrator of *Victory*, on the other hand, is much less sardonically aloof, and proves to be warmly sympathetic to the heroine, Lena.

In *Nostromo*, he is particularly zealous as a coordinator of scenic and thematic ironies. For example, when Nostromo himself is speaking passionately to Giselle Viola, the ubiquitous narrator says that Nostromo is enveloped by a purple and red dusk exactly like that which had enveloped 'the self-destructive passion' of Martin Decoud when he had sat 'no more than fifty yards from that spot'. The narrator also has the implicit character of a philosophical sceptic, for it is he who claims that audacious action and audacious thought lead alike to disillusionment, and it is he who defines love as 'the strongest of illusions'. When he declares that the perennial causes of revolution are 'rooted in the political immaturity of the people, in the indolence of the upper classes and the mental darkness of the lower', we see that he should not be termed 'omniscient', for his own narrative suggests alternative 'roots' of revolution: among them, economic exploitation and social injustice. The implications of his tale may be wiser than the explications by its teller. We should also notice the symbiotic relationship between the narratorial character and the events described: sometimes the doctrines of the narrator seem to be generated by the events, or to have been required as appropriate philosophical 'lubricants' (rationales or explanatory co-ordinators) of the actions in the plot. Again, he is particularly interested in, and romantically responsive to, vistas of natural beauty and majesty: sunsets, seascapes, and the very clouds 'that smoke in stormy trails across the snows of Higuerota'. At other times, by means of implicitly reported thought or speech, his personality may seem to dissolve into that of one of the named characters as that character moves into the foreground. Our recognition of the implicit reportage then restores the distance between narrator and character.

The ubiquitous narrators in Conrad's novels and tales are both less and more than Conrad. 'Less', because Conrad deploys a diversity of such chroniclers as well as a diversity of characters: he creates them and directs them. 'More', because the totality of those impersonal narrators voices a far greater and richer range of views, feelings and attitudes than could be heard in Conrad's letters and non-fictional works: they extend, magnify and diversify their author. Even in the letters, there is an element of conscious characterization: Conrad may dramatize himself as a sceptic when writing to sceptical friends, and as a Christian believer when writing to Christians. In the non-fictional works like *The Mirror of the Sea* and *A Personal Record*, Conrad characterizes himself as a veteran seaman who values that calling, as a former Pole keenly aware of his nation's tragic history, and, throughout, as an eminently civilized, somewhat reserved, devotee of literary art. In his wife's memoirs, a crustier, tetchier, more manic Conrad is depicted. We may thus sense the uselessness of sincerity as a criterion of merit (for a person can be sincerely stupid or sincerely wicked); and, when we consider the scale of creative intelligence manifested by the narration of *Nostromo*, we may appreciate the power of literature to elicit and even generate some of the finest possibilities of the human personality. An imagined ubiquitous narrator may extend, and partly create, the powers of his author.

Part 5 Some Critical Viewpoints

5.1 Contemporaneous Comments

Nostromo was serialized in *T.P.'s Weekly* because the editor, T. P. O'Connor, was enthusiastic about Conrad's works. He may, however, have regretted his decision to publish the novel in his magazine. Years later, Conrad commented on the flyleaf of a copy of the book:

> Serialized in England by TP's Weekly to the special annoyance of its readers who wrote many letters complaining of so much space being taken by utterly unreadable stuff. Fell flat on publication in book form.[1]

The first trade edition of *Nostromo* comprised 3,000 copies for the United States and a further 3,000 for Great Britain and 'the colonies'.[2] Sales were slow and disappointing; eventually, however, after the commercial success of *Chance* in 1914 led to a general rediscovery of Conrad's earlier works, *Nostromo* was reprinted by Dent, Heinemann and Doubleday. In 1926 it was to be filmed (as *The Silver Treasure*) by Fox; and its cinematic qualities were to be appreciated again many years later, when David Lean directed his version.

Conrad's claim that the book initially 'fell flat' underestimates the range of early critical responses, which included very high praise; but certainly the annoyance of the magazine's readers was shared by some reviewers of the book. Predictably, the novel's techniques, particularly the time-shifts, provoked hostility. 'The plot is confused,' said the *British Weekly*; 'the tale does not run smoothly from incident to incident; it is often difficult to say when or where we are.' The *Daily Telegraph* concurred – '[I]t is impossible to feel sure whether the past or the present is being described' – but conceded that '*Nostromo*, although a shapeless work, is yet a shapeless work by a man of genius'. The *Manchester Guardian* encountered 'what seems an arbitrary and baffling design'.[3]

Among Conrad's friends, Cunninghame Graham remarked privately to Edward Garnett that though the book was 'wonderful', the title was misleading: the title should have been *Costaguana*. Since the real interest lay in the depiction of the whole society, the novel should have concluded with Mitchell's monologue instead of narrowing the focus to the deaths of Decoud and Nostromo.[4] A fortnight later, Edward Garnett made similar points when reviewing *Nostromo* in the *Speaker*. He claimed that the psychology of certain characters (Gould, Decoud and Nostromo) was 'not always clear and convincing', but he praised Conrad for his skill in evoking 'the psychology of scene':

[W]e shall see why it is that the artistic imperfections of some of his figures seem of curiously little importance. It is because with most writers the whole illusion of the scene is centred in their characters, but with Mr. Conrad the central illusion is the whole mirage of Nature, in which the figures are, strictly speaking, accessories.[5]

The predominantly laudatory tone of Garnett's characteristically intelligent review was echoed by other commentators; notably by John Buchan in the *Spectator*, who, while acknowledging the formidable difficulty of the text, declared that Conrad 'has a greater range of knowledge – subtle idiomatic knowledge – of the strange ways of the world than any contemporary writer . . . . . [H]e has managed to make clear the strife of ideals in a sordid warfare, and to show the core of seriousness in mock-heroics.' The *Illustrated London News*, noting the 'sweep and breadth in the general design', said: '*Nostromo* will set the seal upon Mr. Conrad's title to rank in the forefront of living novelists.' A coda to these early responses came in 1912, when a fellow-novelist, Arnold Bennett, wrote magnanimously to Conrad:

I read *Higuerota* again not long since. I always think of that book as *Higuerota*, the said mountain being the principal personage in the story. When I first read it I thought it the finest novel of this generation (bar none), and I am still thinking so. It is 'majestic and orbicular' and just peerless, and there's no more to be said. It's the Higuerota among novels.[6]

Cunninghame Graham, Edward Garnett and Arnold Bennett were all shrewd in sensing that the title was misleading. The power of the book, they felt, lay in the creative richness with which Conrad had created so convincing a historic landscape of Costaguana; Nostromo himself is a significant part of that landscape and of the dense clustering of themes, but a part only, and by no means the focal centre that his eponymous role might suggest. Garnett was particularly astute in noting that though there are flaws in the characterization, they do not seem to matter greatly, given the extent to which the characters are 'accessories' (essential accessories, no doubt) to the complex total effect. This matter deserves further consideration.

When Cunninghame Graham grumbled to Conrad about the characterization of Nostromo, the author replied:

I don't defend Nostromo himself. Fact is he does not take my fancy either
. . . . . But truly N is nothing at all – a fiction – embodied vanity of the sailor kind
– a romantic mouthpiece of 'the people' which (I mean 'the people') frequently
experience the very feelings to which he gives utterance. I do not defend him as a
creation.[7]

What this modest apologia emphasizes is the extent to which Conrad
was conceiving characterization thematically and symbolically. As a
psychological entity, Nostromo may be unconvincing; as a contributor
to the large patterns of the novel, psychological, moral, political, he is
amply integrated. At an obvious level, Nostromo serves as one of many
illustrations of the ways in which 'material interests' may be corrupting;
in his fatal fascination by the silver, as we have noted, he is linked
thematically with Gould and with various lesser figures, including the
gringos who allegedly haunt Azuera. In his vanity and concern with self-
image, he illustrates the tendency of individuals (in the fictional society
and in life) to seek a justificative conception of self; so he is linked,
again, with Gould, and, more ironically, with Monygham, who has
made a kind of virtue (a sceptical, bitter integrity) out of his past
disgrace. (Monygham would dispute this, no doubt. When the engineer
says that 'the only solid thing . . . . . is the spiritual value which every one
discovers in his own form of activity', Monygham replies: 'Self-flattery.
Food for that vanity which makes the world go round.')[8] At the time of
Decoud's death, the impersonal narrator even attempts to forge a sym-
metrical parallel between the sophisticated boulevardier and the unsophis-
ticated Capataz: if the former is a 'victim of the disillusioned weariness
which is the retribution meted out to intellectual audacity', the latter is
'victim of the disenchanted vanity which is the reward of audacious
action'.[9] At the historical level, Nostromo, who originally derives great
gratification from serving his masters zealously, but who later feels that
he has been exploited by them (and accordingly betrays his trust and
associates with subversive groups), reflects the larger pattern of social
evolution whereby the workers at first enjoy the paternalistic security
provided by the state's employers but later gain a sense that they have
been exploited and therefore prepare counter-action.

Conrad's symbolic concerns are illustrated by Nostromo's multiple
nomenclature. The Italian word *nostromo* means 'boatswain' (bosun),
and this character was indeed a bosun on his arrival in Sulaco; but the

main ironies surrounding his name depend on the more obvious fact that 'Nostromo' is an abbreviation of the Italian phrase *nostro uomo*, 'our man': which proclaims his identity as one who prides himself on his indispensability to his masters. There is heavy irony when, having betrayed his trust, he becomes known as 'Captain Fidanza', for *fidanza* is Italian for 'trust' or 'fidelity'. (There may be a hint of *fidanzato*, fiancé, for he becomes betrothed during that final phase.) Even his Christian name, Gian' Battista (John-the-Baptist), may have been chosen for its ironic connotations: John the Baptist was an 'usher-in' of Christianity; Decoud calls Nostromo 'this active usher-in of the material implements for our progress'.[10] So, in such ways, Conrad has adroitly made Nostromo the bearer of a large symbolic and thematic burden. The weaknesses in the characterization lie, firstly, in the dialogue, as we have seen: for Nostromo tends to speak in a theatrical, even melodramatic way; and both the descriptions and the dialogue at the time of Nostromo's infatuation with Giselle seem to derive from conventional and second-rate romantic fiction. Conrad may have borrowed phrases from Anatole France, but France did not write at his best in such scenes. Secondly, the narratorial analyses of his vanity and of his 'fall' often seem over-elaborate, as though providing needlessly weighty explanations of the simple.

In the case of Decoud, Cunninghame Graham's doubts again seem valid. As Albert Guerard later pointed out,[11] the narratorial hostility directed against Decoud often seems greater than he deserves; there is a disparity between his actions, which seem predominantly admirable, and the narrator's persistent emphasis on his hollow cynicism. His sceptical view of the world around him is largely (though not totally) supported by the text; the burgeoning of his love for Antonia and of his reluctant commitment to politics makes a credible combination; so the narrator sometimes appears to be attacking a different, more egoistic and superficial figure than the one whom we have observed. Perhaps Conrad was punishing rather too severely a scepticism which (as the letters to Cunninghame Graham show) was a deeply ingrained part of his own depressive temperament. Another possibility is that since some of the judgements applied to Decoud have been borrowed from Anatole France's verdict on Prosper Mérimée, the disparity between the judgements and the characterization stems from inadequate assimilation of source-materials. The fact remains that, in his intelligence, clear-sightedness and connoisseurship of absurdities, Decoud often stands in a closer relationship to the impersonal narrator than does any of the other characters.

That the title of *Nostromo* is a misnomer seems to have been acknowledged by Conrad himself, in a letter of 1923:

I will take the liberty to point out that *Nostromo* has never been intended for the hero of the Tale of the Seaboard. Silver is the pivot of the moral and material events, affecting the lives of everybody in the tale. That this was my deliberate purpose there can be no doubt. I struck the first note of my intention in the unusual form which I gave to the title of the First Part, by calling it 'The Silver of the Mine,' and by telling the story of the enchanted treasure on Azuera, which, strictly speaking, has nothing to do with the rest of the novel. The word 'silver' occurs almost at the very beginning of the story proper, and I took care to introduce it in the very last paragraph, which would perhaps have been better without the phrase which contains that key-word.[12]

So, whether the novel should be called *Costaguana*, *Higuerota*, *Silver*, or, after all, *Nostromo*, is a problem worth pondering; for the effect of the pondering is to make one more aware of the text's enormous richness in thematic scale and scope. It is difficult to imagine any brief title which would not, in some way, understate the range of the novel thus heralded.

5.2 F. R. Leavis

In the 1930s there seems to have been a decline in Conrad's reputation, as younger generations of writers (among them, D. H. Lawrence, T. S. Eliot, Aldous Huxley, W. H. Auden) came to the forefront of discussion. Elizabeth Bowen remarked in 1936: 'Conrad is in abeyance. We are not clear yet how to rank him; there is an uncertain pause.'[13]

As though to end that 'uncertain pause' and provide clear guidance about 'how to rank him', the Cambridge lecturer, F. R. Leavis, published in his periodical *Scrutiny* (June and October 1941) the influential articles which were to be reprinted in *The Great Tradition*, 1948. 'Conrad', said Leavis, 'is among the very greatest novelists in the language – or any language.' In this account, Conrad stood alongside George Eliot, Henry James and D. H. Lawrence as one of the giants in 'the great tradition' of novelists distinguished by 'a vital capacity for experience, a kind of reverent openness before life, and a marked moral intensity'. *Nostromo* was emphatically presented as a masterpiece; its strengths being the luxuriant magnificence of the evocation of exotic life and colour, and, more importantly, 'the way in which the whole book forms a rich and subtle but highly organized pattern . . . . .; the pattern is one of moral significances'.

Critical Studies: Nostromo

The impressiveness is not a matter of any profundity of search into human experience, or any explorative subtlety in the analysis of human behaviour. It is a matter rather of the firm and vivid concreteness with which the representative attitudes and motives are realized, and the rich economy of pattern that plays them off against one another.

Even the melodramatic features, Leavis claimed, were controlled by that 'pattern of moral significance', and thus maintained the 'robust vigour' of Elizabethan drama.[14]

In his later years, and particularly after his death in 1978, Leavis's outlook was widely criticized. That 'great tradition', which yoked together writers as heterogeneous as Jane Austen and D. H. Lawrence, was rightly seen as a rather specious invention; while the liberal moralism invoked by Leavis was treated by some left-wingers as at best questionable and at worst élitist and therefore reactionary. So it is worth recalling that in his time, Leavis was in various ways a radical rejuvenator of literary studies; a teacher who gave a new prestige and intensity to the criticism of literature, and who for decades influenced the choice of texts in schools and universities; an arbiter whose findings, if controversial, provided a basis for many subsequent assessments of the writers in question. After *The Great Tradition* and the later Conradian studies published in *'Anna Karenina' and Other Essays*, Conrad in general and *Nostromo* in particular could not be ignored or treated dismissively by professional critics or teachers at large.

5.3 Left-Wing Views

Given that in *Nostromo* Conrad shows not just an awareness, but a shrewdly critical awareness, of the Marxist conception of history, the views of left-wing critics are particularly pertinent. Arnold Kettle, in *An Introduction to the English Novel* (1953) offered an enthusiastic tribute to *Nostromo*. Some of his points were close to Leavis's, particularly in his emphasis on the stupendous scale and complexity of organization of the work. He also, like Leavis (who in turn had been anticipated by Cunninghame Graham in this respect), saw analogies in character-portrayal between Conrad and the Elizabethan dramatists.

Conrad's method is to over-simplify somewhat individual character in the sense of giving each individual very sharply-defined personal characteristics, frequently reiterated, so that each stands out clearly, not only in contrast to the others, but against the clear, concrete, surface-objective background of the whole . . . . . In fact, of course, the characters are not simple at all: by the end of the book their depths and complexities are well established; it is their presentation which is simplified. Like the Elizabethan dramatists, Conrad employs his own convention for the revelation of social life.[15]

Kettle praises Conrad's political insight, particularly into the 'inadequacy of liberalism', and remarks that the view of history offered in *Nostromo* is precisely that of Engels in the following letter:

History makes itself in such a way that the final result always arises from conflicts between many individual wills, of which each again has been made what it is by a host of particular conditions of life. Thus there are innumerable intersecting forces, an infinite series of parallelograms of forces which give rise to one resultant – the historical event. This again may itself be viewed as the product of a power which, taken as a whole, works *unconsciously* and without volition. For what each individual wills is obstructed by everyone else, and what emerges is something that no one ever willed.[16]

(Conrad, however, might object that one does not have to be a Marxist to see this; indeed, as we have noted, Adam Smith had made much the same point in his *Wealth of Nations*.)

Kettle offers one complaint about *Nostromo*. Conrad repeatedly uses the phrase 'material interest' [*sic*] instead of using the term 'imperialism', and there is an associated vagueness:

The implication begins to creep in . . . . . that something in the very nature of things, something beyond human control (yet never defined), is responsible for the tragedy of *Nostromo*.[17]

The reader may well object that Kettle is wrong to say: 'Objectively it is clear that "material interest" stands for imperialism.' The functionality of the phrase (which should actually be a plural, 'material interests') lies in its plurality of connotations. Imperialism is certainly one of those connotations; capitalism is another. But there are others: avarice; materialism; concern with matter; and still others, more specific and less abstract: finance-houses, merchants, bankers, investors, speculators, entrepreneurs. And the central potency of the phrase lies in the specific irony with which this literary context invests it, and which transforms it from being a mere journalistic cliché of those times into a peculiarly potent coordinator of the book's themes. 'Material interests', in *Nostromo*, reminds us not only of the varying forms of materialism, capitalism and imperialism which are assailing Costaguana; it reminds us also of the whole endeavour by men to impose their wills on the material environment; it reminds us of the vast irony that the strivings of men seem ephemeral when measured by that global time-scale suggested so potently by the massive serenity of Mount Higuerota and the vast Cordilleras. Kettle complains that there is an implication 'that something in the very nature of things, something beyond human control (yet never defined) is responsible for the tragedy . . . . .' Yet the definitions are there in the text. The things 'beyond human control' are human myopia and egotism, and the sheer brevity of human life. One of the reasons for the memorable potency of the central nightscape, of that sequence in which Decoud, on the lighter, moves through utter blackness, is that it provides a mnemonic of the annihilation that awaits us all: an annihilation of the individual and, perhaps, of the human race. No wonder that Kettle, as a Marxist materialist, develops a blind spot when the implications of 'material interests' are extended by Conrad.

A later Marxist, Terry Eagleton, exploited in his *Criticism and Ideology* (1976) the 'deconstructive' notion that literary texts are riven with contradictions which are symptomatic of ideological contradictions within strife-torn society. One Conradian contradiction is that between the appeal of organicism (the closed, tightly knit, organic community) and Romantic individualism (which gives supremacy to the individual ego). Affirmation is repeatedly undermined by scepticism. Therefore:

At the centre of each of Conrad's works is a resonant silence . . . . .
The absent centre of *Nostromo* is in part Nostromo himself, but also the silver of which he is the agent . . . . . As the determining structure of which the novel's characters are the bearers . . . . ., the silver is the unifying principle of the entire action; but since that action has for Conrad no historical intelligibility, it is a principle which must of necessity be dramatically absent . . . . .
The need for value, and the recognition of its utter vacuity: it is here that the deepest contradiction of Conrad's enterprise, one integral to the imperialist ideology he shared, stands revealed.[18]

The reader may reflect that Conrad certainly voiced contradiction, and, as *homo duplex*, was well aware of the fact. In a letter to the *New York Times* (1901), he wrote:

The only legitimate basis of creative work lies in the courageous recognition of all the irreconcilable antagonisms that make our life so enigmatic, so burdensome, so fascinating, so dangerous – so full of hope. They exist! And this is the only fundamental truth of fiction.[19]

Certainly, Eagleton is right to see in Conrad an extreme tension between affirmation and scepticism. In *Nostromo*, Mrs Gould is sympathetically presented as an affirmer and source of value; yet Decoud is persuasively presented as the voice of a penetrating scepticism. The suggestion, however, that Conrad is thereby in deep complicity with 'imperialist ideology' seems curiously unfair to an author who raised questions, and voiced the contradictions, which it is allegedly the aim of imperialists to stifle and to conceal. To say that 'the entire action' in Costaguana 'has for Conrad no historical intelligibility' is a rather negative way of noting that in *Nostromo* Conrad is concerned to challenge the notion of 'historical intelligibility' by depicting rival 'intelligibilities' and questioning their adequacy: Eagleton seems to be trying to teach his grandmother to suck hollow eggs. As a matter of textual accuracy, his assertion that the silver is 'dramatically absent' seems quite incorrect. Whether it's filling the lighter in the gulf, weighting the pockets of Decoud as he sinks under the waves, constituting Viola's spectacle-frames or Nostromo's whistle and buttons, silver is ubiquitously present, and the process of extracting silver bullion from the rough ore is carefully specified by the narrator in Part I, Chapter 8. There *are* ideologically revealing gaps and hollows in various works of Conrad (the invisible, unspecified cargo of the ship in *The Nigger of the 'Narcissus'*, for example), but the silver in *Nostromo* is very tangibly present.

Perhaps misgivings about this matter were in Eagleton's mind when he later described Chapter 4 of his book (the chapter containing the discussion of Conrad) as marred by 'inexact formulation, metaphorical gesture, partial and reductive reading';[20] nevertheless, his discussion has the provocative verve of bold concision.

In 1981 a popular American critic, Fredric Jameson, claimed in *The Political Unconscious* that *Nostromo* 'accredits the good opinion the industrial West has of itself' by showing that the South American people, being 'lazy' and 'shiftless', need to have order imposed on them from abroad; furthermore, Conrad's conservatism is demonstrated by the fact that 'the Blancos are good, the Monteristas evil'.[21] Jameson overlooks one consistent feature of Conrad's novels and tales: outsiders who seek to impose order on a foreign area usually make matters worse rather than better: this is true of Lingard's area of Borneo (in *Almayer's Folly* and *An Outcast of the Islands*), of the Congo (as depicted in 'An Outpost of Progress' and 'Heart of Darkness'), of Sumatra's Patusan (in *Lord Jim*), and, if Monygham and Mrs Gould are to be believed, of Sulaco. It's true that Colonel Sotillo, the Montero brothers and their followers Gamacho and Fuentes are depicted sardonically and satirically; but the Blancos, the aristocratic landowners, are presented variously as anachronistic, naïvely idealistic, vacillating, craven, ineffectual and enfeebled. Consider Decoud's account of Don Juste López, the temporizing President of the Provincial Assembly:

'Don Juste Lopez had had half his beard singed off at the muzzle of a trabuco loaded with slugs, of which every one missed him, providentially. And as he turned his head from side to side it was exactly as if there had been two men inside his frock-coat, one nobly whiskered and solemn, the other untidy and scared.'[22]

The text offers a finely ironic and historically astute account of the Provincial Assembly's rationalization (as hopeful pragmatism) of its abject surrender to superior force; and this is only one instance of the many ways in which the text's complexity challenges Jameson's schematization.

Another influential critic in (and of) the United States was Edward Said, who, over the years, gave extensive attention to Conrad. In the essay 'Through Gringo Eyes' (*Harper's*, April 1988), Said claimed that although Conrad astutely sees imperialism as 'doomed by impossible ambition', he nevertheless 'writes as a man in whom a *Western* view of the non-Western world is so deeply ingrained that it blinds him to other histories, other cultures, other aspirations'. Therefore:

Conrad was both an anti-imperialist and an imperialist – progressive when it came to rendering the self-confirming, self-deluding corruption of the West's colonial drive; reactionary in his inability to imagine that Costaguana could ever have had a meaningful existence of its own, which the imperialists had violently disturbed. But lest we think patronizingly of Conrad as merely the creature of his own time, we had better note that we today appear to show no particular advance on his views.[23]

The reader may sense that, once again, *Nostromo* displays a tenacious capacity to criticize its critics. Far from suggesting that Costaguana could never have had 'a meaningful existence of its own', the novel emphasizes that the known history of Costaguana has repeatedly been an *imposed* history: the story of Costaguana is one of recurrent invasion, conquest, exploitation; it is the victors, not the victims, who tend to be the historians of any region. Conrad emphasizes that the reign of the new imperialists is just one phase in that long process of imposition. The very first chapter of the novel draws attention to the former era of Spanish rule, and frequent ironic analogies link the old and new *conquistadores*. The novel's rich social panorama does not neglect the indigenous inhabitants: in many vivid descriptive paragraphs their plight is shown. When the first chapter tells us that the poor 'associat[e] by an obscure instinct of consolation the ideas of evil and wealth', it cites a notion that the ensuing narrative will amply validate. Edward Said's argument actually seems to repeat, without due acknowledgement, the case made forcefully at several points in the novel: for instance, by Decoud in Part II, Chapter 5. There Decoud recalls the days when Sir Francis Drake, in the service of English speculators, plundered the town:

'In those days this town was full of wealth. Those men came to take it. Now the whole land is like a treasure-house, and all these people are breaking into it, whilst we are cutting each other's throats. The only thing that keeps them out is mutual jealousy. But they'll come to an agreement some day – and by the time we've settled our quarrels and become decent and honourable, there'll be nothing left for us. It has always been the same. We are a wonderful people, but it has always been our fate to be' – he did not say 'robbed,' but added, after a pause – 'exploited!'[24]

Giorgio Viola makes a similar point when Decoud says: 'We are all for the people – in the end.' He replies: 'Yes . . . . . And meantime they fight for you. Blind. Esclavos! [Slaves!]' Adroitly, the text later satirizes a related xenophobia when Gamacho advocates war 'against France, England, Germany, and the United States, who . . . . . aimed at robbing poor people of their lands'.[25]

Said suggests that Conrad ignores the rights of the 'natives'; but *Nostromo* soon makes clear that to define the 'natives' is no easy matter, given that the population is already a 'melting-pot of nations': the social mixture includes the Indians, who so often serve as the hapless workforce; mulattos; people of European, particularly Spanish, ancestry; many people descended from a mixture of Spanish and Indian forebears (the mestizos); and a newer influx of Italians, Britons and North Americans. The very 'patriots' who urge the people to cast out foreign exploiters bear foreign (Spanish) names: Montero, Gamacho, Fuentes, Sotillo. Nor does Conrad sentimentalize the pre-colonial era as a Golden Age: Decoud remarks that in 'old times', 'the persistent barbarism of our native continent did not wear the black coats of politicians, but went about yelling, half-naked, with bows and arrows in its hands'.[26] If the history of Costaguana has been so turbulently unstable as to suggest, at times, a black comedy or savage farce, it is little different in this respect from the actual history of Argentina, Paraguay, Colombia, Venezuela and other strife-torn republics; and, as we have seen, the depredations of the fictional Guzmán Bento were based on, and in some respects exceeded by, historic dictators like José da Francia and Francísco Solano López of Paraguay. As Edward Said notes, the text reminds us that even the great liberator of South America, Simón Bolívar, eventually made the despairing statement:

America is ungovernable; those who have served her revolution have ploughed in the sea. These countries will inevitably fall into the hands of the unrestrained multitude, to become then the prey of petty tyrants of all grades and races . . . . .[27]

By a wealth of details, *Nostromo* implies the history which lacks its historian: the story of the common masses. One telling detail comes when Viola is observing the discipline of the new recruits in the army of Barrios:

One-eyed Barrios and his officers had done wonders with the recruits in a short time. Those Indios, only caught the other day, had gone swinging past in double quick time, like bersaglieri; they looked well fed, too, and had whole uniforms. 'Uniforms!' he repeated with a half-smile of pity.[28]

The telling detail here is the phrase, 'only caught the other day': the Indians may be contented enough, well-fed and in new uniforms; but they have effectively been captured, to fight perhaps to the death, to guard the dividends of investors based in San Francisco and London. The lethal price exacted by material progress is instanced in particulars like this:

A fire of broken furniture out of the Intendencia saloons, mostly gilt, was burning on the Plaza, in a high flame swaying right upon the statue of Charles IV. The dead body of a man was lying on the steps of the pedestal, his arms thrown wide open, and his sombrero covering his face – the attention of some friend, perhaps.[29]

The juxtaposition is typical of Conrad's tirelessly ironic imagination: here, an unknown victim of the revolutionary upheaval lies at the foot of the stony image of the figure chronicled by orthodox historians.

Edward Said says that, in one important respect, later writers like Graham Greene and V. S. Naipaul have followed Conrad's unfortunate example:

When there is something indigenous to be described, it is, following Conrad, unutterably corrupt, degenerate, irredeemable.[30]

To this charge, one answer is provided by the descriptive sequence in Part I, Chapter 8, in which Don Pepe, the overseer of the mine's workforce, is contrasted with Mrs Gould. To her, the miners look all alike; but Pepe prides himself on his individual knowledge of them. Whole families, we are told, had travelled from afar to seek the work and security of the mine:

Father first, in a pointed straw hat, then the mother with the bigger children, generally also a diminutive donkey, all under burdens, except the leader himself, or perhaps some grown girl, the pride of the family, stepping barefooted and straight as an arrow, with braids of raven hair, a thick, haughty profile, and no load to carry but the small guitar of the country and a pair of soft leather sandals tied together across her back.[31]

It is difficult to see here any evidence of the 'unutterably corrupt, degenerate [and] irredeemable'. In this sequence one irony is, of course, that these people are heading not only to employment, food and apparent security, but also to regimentation: the miners will have to wear green uniforms, and these families will be accommodated in identical villages with the utilitarian names 'Village One, Village Two, Village Three'. Pepe's endeavour to know the workers as individuals is in conflict with the institutionalizing tendencies of the organization he serves, an organization which seeks to render into a regimented and conforming mass so many disparate figures. *Nostromo* vividly and variously displays salient socio-economic factors that were to be elaborately postulated and documented by subsequent notable socio-economic analysts (Max Weber, Georg Simmel and R. H. Tawney, among others) and by popular sociologists (like David Riesman and William Whyte).

In short, far from being unable to see life beyond the parameters of imperialism, Conrad has generally anticipated Said by showing very precisely and critically the mechanisms whereby imperialism seeks 'to impose its "narrative" – its authorship, plots, and themes – on Latin America (and elsewhere)'.[32] Certainly a pessimistic circularity may be seen in the book's explicit political theses. In contrast to 'the development of material interests', we are offered a recommendation of 'the continuity and the force that can be found only in a moral principle'; but, to be effective, that moral principle must become political action; and political action (the novel insists) tends to corrupt the moral ideals. Another thesis is that the power of international or multinational business corporations eludes or surmounts national democratic control; those who pay the piper call the tune. There is enough historic truth in these theses to make socialists hesitate; but possibly there is enough historic truth in the indictment of capitalism to help them to overcome the hesitation. We may doubt that literary works have ever exerted much political influence; yet the fact of literary censorship by governments may suggest the contrary; and some of Conrad's writings are still banned in Poland, his homeland.

Part 6   Conclusion: Pleasures of the Text

The world is a comedy to those that think, a tragedy to those that feel.
                                        Horace Walpole, letter of 16 August 1776

Nostromo is a strenuous, demanding, perceptive and profound work, raising grave questions about history, politics, human evolution and human identity. Understandably, critics commonly address themselves to the serious issues it raises; they comment on its plausibility or veracity in these areas. This understandable response may, however, entail a failure to respect adequately the fact that *Nostromo* is a work of fiction: it belongs to a *genre* which, first and foremost, succeeds if it entertains. The novel is not a political manifesto or a treatise on economics; it offers imaginative pleasure. To say this is not to trivialize it; on the contrary. Stupid entertainments please stupid people; intelligent entertainments please intelligent people. What gives *Nostromo* its staying-power while other texts fade into oblivion is largely that its creative intelligence enables it to sustain multiple readings over a long period of time; its obliquities, ambiguities, ironies and paradoxes provide sophisticated satisfactions, even though many features of the narrative offer graphically immediate rewards. The ironies of the text are innumerable, ranging from those vast in scale to those which are a matter of tiny details of phrasing. Some of them may seem bleak, even appalling, in their implications, but to perceive irony (even tragic irony) is to engage a faculty related to one's sense of humour, for one thereby detects connections which elude others; one sees how circumstances ambush and mock the unsuspecting; one senses that the mechanism of tragedy often has disturbing similarities to the mechanism of farce. Marx alleged that a historical event occurs first as tragedy but later recurs as farce;[1] Conrad's janiform vision enables him to see a given event as simultaneously tragic and farcical. Similarly, Conrad has a keen sense of absurdity; and the absurd can be both grave (as when it stems from an incongruity between laudable human aspirations and an unresponsive universe) and comical (as when there is a ludicrous disparity between pompous posture and demeaning situation). An enduring literary text sets a complex series of puzzles: puzzles to be solved both by further scrutiny of its details and by our recollections of the world around us.

106

In summary, *Nostromo*'s story of human affairs may seem bleak and depressing; in the detail of its rendering, its story may well seem exhilarating. Most obviously, this is because it has many passages infused with the spirit of comedy, a comedy now gentle, now satiric, now farcical. The gentle comedy is frequently present in the depiction of pompous Captain Mitchell and in the manner of his observations. The narrator reports his account of Ribiera's entry on a lame mule:

> The animal, moreover, expired under him at the end of the Alameda, where the military band plays sometimes in the evenings between the revolutions.[2]

The joke lies partly in the mimicry of a portentous style ('The animal . . . . . expired') and in the contrast between dignified literary phrasing and a ludicrous visual image (frightened dictator falling off a collapsing mule). It lies partly in the ambiguous phrasing of the reference to the band's performances: Mitchell perhaps means that in the months or years between revolutions, the band plays each evening; but the phrasing invites us to envisage the grotesque possibility that revolutions are so frequent that only one evening elapses between each of them. Again, when Mitchell (in Part III, Chapter 10) is informing his young visitor about the great events which established the republic of Sulaco, there's a complex serio-comic effect. What Mitchell says is of interest to us, because (though he may misjudge some matters) he supplies crucial information about the fates of various characters; but we are also aware that for his visitor, who understands little of Mitchell's account ('the abominable Pedrito! Who was he?'), the day must have been one of excruciating tedium, with Mitchell's monologue extending all day and half the night.

A broader, more satirical kind of comedy is present in the depiction of various rebel leaders: General Montero, his brother Pedrito, Colonel Sotillo, and the garrulous orators Gamacho and Fuentes: all of them, in different ways, avaricious, hypocritical, pretentious and naïve. Frequently, when these characters are in the foreground, our reading conventions modulate markedly from those which apply when Giorgio Viola or Charles Gould are to the fore; our conventions approximate to those which are appropriate when we read a satiric farce: we curb our expectation of subtle realism and ask only that the exaggeration of common features of vice or folly be lively and adroit. An obvious instance in the text occurs when Sotillo hastily climbs, fully dressed, into his hammock in order to feign illness to an unwelcome visitor; having done so, he leaps out of the hammock:

His spurs having become entangled in a perfect welter of ponchos, he nearly pitched on his head, and did not recover his balance till the middle of the room.[3]

A subtler comedy of manners is shown when Don José Avellanos feels courteously obliged to drink Mrs Gould's tea, which he detests:

He drank up all the tea at once in one draught. This performance was invariably followed by a slight shudder and a low involuntary 'br-r-r-r,' which was not covered by the hasty exclamation, 'Excellent!'[4]

On a larger scale, the portrayal of Don José Avellanos illustrates the 'jocoserious' effect of the ironic handling of characters. In one perspective he is tragic: a well-meaning, idealistic, aristocratic figure who has suffered for his country, strives in his writings and speeches for its regeneration, and dies disappointed as the Ribiera regime collapses. In another, cooler perspective, he's an anachronistic, quixotic figure, unable to see the glaring disparity between his abstract talk of national honour and the quagmire of avarice and ambition which constitutes much of the continuing history of the land.

A pervasive kind of pleasure offered by the text will be that savoured by linguistic sensualists – by readers with an ear for sensuous rhetorical effects (alliteration, assonance, rhythmic patterns) and for artfully varied modes of discourse, ranging from the coarsely colloquial to the lyrically romantic. Sometimes the prose is self-effacingly 'transparent': it seems proficiently functional and does not attract attention to itself. Frequently, on the other hand, we recognize that while telling us of events in the fictional world, the impersonal narrator is also choosing his words carefully to offer us an augmentary auditory pleasure. Examples are innumerable. During a battle:

Tall trails of dust subsided here and there. In a speckless sky the sun hung clear and blinding.[5]

We may not consciously recognize the stylistic devices, but our sense of the scene is accompanied by a sense of artfully patterned discourse: the prose, self-aware, begins to sing with alliteration ('Tall trails', 'dust subsided . . . . . blinding', 'speckless sky the sun') , with assonance ('here . . . . . clear', 'subsided . . . . . blinding', 'dust . . . . . sun hung') and with rhythm: each of these quoted sentences has a firm metrical base of iambic pentameter. The subliminal effect of such sound-patterning is to create in us the intuition that the narrator values words not only as functional tools for conveying a quantity of information but also as instruments of subtly sensuous gratification. Our impression of Conrad's civilized, deliberate poise derives in part from that subliminal awareness of a poetic valuing of language; which, in turn, smuggles one of the novel's subtlest political implications – the commendation of civilized care and sensitivity. Furthermore, the text is proleptically cinematic: before the film industry had emerged from its clumsy infancy, *Nostromo* was offering panoramic scenic vistas, startling montages, zoom-shots, crafty angles, expressive lighting and colour, an epic scale and meticulous close-ups.

The adroit interplay of the vast and the tiny, the general and the particular, the concrete and the abstract, is a feature of much major literary work. One reason for the richness of *Nostromo* is that Conrad likes to extend the extremes: that is to say, when he is concretely specific he is very minutely so, and when he offers the abstract or generalized he is often very quotably and epigrammatically so; the two extremes thus form patterns of mutually reinforcing contrasts. Frequently, a disparity between the two is a source of irony, as in this juxtaposition of Viola's execration of tyranny and his culinary misfortunes:

[U]nder the walls of Gaeta, tyranny would have expired for ever had it not been for that accursed Piedomontese race of kings and ministers. When sometimes a frying-pan caught fire during a delicate operation with some shredded onions, and the old man was seen backing out of the doorway, swearing and coughing violently in an acrid cloud of smoke, the name of Cavour – the arch intriguer sold to kings and tyrants – could be heard involved in imprecations against the China girls, cooking in general, and the brute of a country where he was reduced to live for the love of liberty that traitor had strangled.[6]

The detail, 'backing out of the doorway', is acutely realistic, as experimentation will show you: if you go out of a doorway forwards with a burning frying-pan, the draught blows the smoke back into your face. The comedy here is not merely at the expense of Viola, whose lofty political ideals are contrasted with his incompetence at the mundane task of frying onions; it has a more general resonance, for one of the tragicomic themes of the book is the perennial tendency of human ideals to be mocked by our mundane situations: we have imaginations that can dream and conceptualize, but also bellies that groan to be fed – and bodies that stumble and blunder.

We tend to evaluate literary works by moral standards (which include the political). Our response to the implicit moral recommendations in a novel is, however, greatly complicated by our aesthetic awareness: by our knowledge that we have been undergoing a voluntary and hypothetical experience. It is hypothetical because the bullets in the story do not really wound; the blood has not really flowed; so that a killing which would horrify us in actuality may gratify us (as a source of imaginative excitement) in the reading. We have thus been engaged with morality and politics 'in quotation marks'. While comparing the fiction with our memory of actuality (a constant process), we are doubtless learning more about actuality; and our outlooks are being modified, if only in some infinitesimal degree. But there exists no device, no encephalograph, which can tell us precisely the extent to which our sense of imaginative escape from actuality (our 'immersion' in the imaginary world) is outweighed, if indeed it is outweighed at all, by our sense that searching and transforming questions have been directed outwards towards that familiar actuality (in a scrutiny of the real world). The satisfyingly vivid descriptive texture of *Nostromo* may make it more seductively escapist or more challengingly probing. One of the grand paradoxes of the work, then, is that while seeming to teach us much about historical actualities, it seduces us into imaginative holiday in a far-off land created between the ears of Joseph Conrad as he sat at his English desk; yet the seduction depends on recognizable if surprising connections between the imaginary and the familiar.

Finally, the value of the text lies not in its paraphrasable themes or messages, however worthy they may be, but in our experience of its totality; the total embodiment. Commentary can only be reductive if it is regarded as a substitute for that embodiment; it can only be enhancive if it directs the reader back with greater responsiveness to Conrad's words. The distinctive knowledge provided by a good novel like *Nostromo* is merely – but supremely – the knowledge that only a good novel can provide. It may, however, lead us to reflect that, as social beings, we are inscribed by the author whose pseudonym is authority. In a novel, the better the author, the more independent may seem the characters. In the book of life, the more skilful the authority, the more the people may gain the illusion of sufficient independence. Literary texts provide excellent material for one of the most important cultural studies: the study of the extent to which all of us are cultural artefacts, who, with different social authors, different authorities, could be different characters in different social stories, perhaps worse, but perhaps better. Major novels remind us that, for centuries, society has inscribed women with submissive characterization; and that, as a result, millions of women have led half-lives. Similarly, for centuries, society has inscribed men with aggressive characterization; and, as a result, millions of men have died on battlefields. The study of fiction is increasingly becoming recognized as the study of social authorship. Texts like *Nostromo* offer paradigms – conspicuous models – of social inscription, and they offer warnings about such inscription. They extend the definition of the human self. And, by their constant and proper resistance to exhaustive interpretation (given that an interpretation of a text can never be equivalent to our experience of that text), they constantly champion the defiant, if frustrated, inner life of us all: that inner life which no known social system can ever fully liberate, precisely because one blessing and one curse of being human is that we can always imagine ourselves as characters in a better story than any which is available here and now.

Part 7 Caudal

7.1 Notes

The following abbreviations are used:

CLJC   *The Collected Letters of Joseph Conrad*, ed. Frederick R. Karl and Laurence Davies (Cambridge: Cambridge University Press. Vol. I, 1983; Vol. II, 1986; Vol. III, 1988).

CPB   *Conrad's Polish Background: Letters to and from Polish Friends*, ed. Zdzisław Najder (London: Oxford University Press, 1964).

CWW   Norman Sherry: *Conrad's Western World* (London: Cambridge University Press, 1971).

JB   Jocelyn Baines: *Joseph Conrad: A Critical Biography* (London: Weidenfeld & Nicolson, 1960).

JCC   Zdzisław Najder: *Joseph Conrad: A Chronicle* (Cambridge: Cambridge University Press, 1983).

LCG   *Joseph Conrad's Letters to R. B. Cunninghame Graham*, ed. Cedric Watts (London: Cambridge University Press, 1969).

LL   *Joseph Conrad: Life & Letters*, written and edited by G. Jean-Aubry (2 volumes; London: Heinemann, 1927).

PART 2 (pp. 3–18)

1. *CPB*, p. 240.
2. *Some Reminiscences* (London: Nash, 1912), p. 18.
3. 'human affairs': *Some Reminiscences*, p. 19; 'anarchism': 'Author's Note' to *The Secret Agent* (London: Dent, 1947), p. ix; 'Society': *CLJC* II, p. 160.
4. *CLJC*, II, p. 30; *CLJC*, II, p. 17; *Notes on Life and Letters* (London: Dent, 1949), p. 8.
5. Conrad anticipates Modernism by the radicalism of outlook and technique in 'Heart of Darkness' and *Nostromo*, for instance; and he anticipates Deconstructionism (which cherishes contradictions) by his janiformity and linguistic scepticism.
6. *CPB*, p. 5.
7. *LL*, I, p. 16.
8. 'Author's Note' to *A Personal Record* (London: Dent, 1946), p. viii.
9. *JCC*, p. 29.
10. *LL*, II, pp. 321–2.
11. *The Mirror of the Sea* (London: Dent, 1946), p. 162.

112

12. *CWW*, pp. 163–8, 420.
13. *CPB*, p. 176. The subsequent three small-type quotations are from pp. 176–8.
14. *CPB*, p. 88.
15. *Joseph Conrad: A Personal Remembrance* (London: Duckworth, 1924), pp. 57–8.
16. *CLJC*, II, p. 230.
17. JCC, p. 54.
18. *Last Essays* (London: Dent, 1955), p. 13.
19. Report of the Court of Inquiry, reprinted in Norman Sherry's *Conrad's Eastern World* (London: Cambridge University Press, 1966), pp. 297–8.
20. *Last Essays*, p. 17.
21. B. R. Mitchell and P. Deane: *Abstract of British Historical Statistics* (London: Cambridge University Press, 1962), p. 218. E. Blackmore: *The British Mercantile Marine* (London: Griffin, 1897), pp. 134–5.
22. John Gross: *The Rise and Fall of the Man of Letters* (London: Weidenfeld & Nicolson), p. 199.
23. See Cedric Watts: *The Deceptive Text: An Introduction to Covert Plots* (Brighton: Harvester, 1984), Chapter 5.
24. *Spectator*, 19 October 1895, p. 530; *Manchester Guardian* (reviewing *An Outcast*), 19 May 1896, p. 5.
25. *Letters from Conrad 1895 to 1924*, ed. Edward Garnett (London: Nonesuch, 1927), p. 225.
26. *Joseph Conrad: Letters to William Blackwood and David S. Meldrum*, ed. William Blackburn (Durham, NC: Duke University Press, 1958), p. 192.
27. *LL*, II, p. 94.
28. *JCC*, p. 276.
29. *CLJC*, III, p. 257; *JCC*, pp. 275–6.
30. JB, p. 350.
31. 'Introduction' to *The Good Soldier* (London: Heinemann, 1970), p. 11.

PART 3 (pp. 19–51)

1. *CLJC*, II, p. 448.
2. *CLJC*, III, p. 6 *et passim*.
3. *CLJC*, III, pp. 158–9.
4. 'Author's Note' to *Nostromo* (London: Dent, 1918), p. ix.
5. ibid., p. xiii.
6. John Halverson and Ian Watt: 'The Original Nostromo: Conrad's Source', *Review of English Studies*, NS, X (1959), pp. 49–52.
7. *CWW*, p. 164.
8. *Nostromo* (London and New York: Harper, 1904), pp. 306, 145.
9. JB, pp. 313–14.
10. See Cedric Watts and Laurence Davies: *Cunninghame Graham: A Critical Biography* (Cambridge: Cambridge University Press, 1979).

Critical Studies: Nostromo

[3]The notes below.

11. *LCG*, p. 145; *LL*, II, pp. 321–2.
12. *LCG*, p. 37.
13. *Times*, 8 October 1852, p. 5.
14. *A Vanished Arcadia* (London: Heinemann, 1901), p. 286.
15. *CWW*, p. 149.
16. *Cunninghame Graham: A Critical Biography*, p. 26.
17. *Thirteen Stories* (London: Heinemann, 1900), pp. 60–61.
18. *Hope* (London: Duckworth, 1910), p. 123.
19. *Brought Forward* (London: Duckworth, 1916), p. 175.
20. *LCG*, p. 155; *T.P.'s Weekly*, IV, p. 327.
21. *LCG*, p. 208.
22. 'The Enemy' in *Justice*, 3 May 1913, p. 5.
23. *LCG*, p. 152.
24. *CLJC*, III, p. 28.
25. A. Dumas: *Mémoires de Garibaldi* (Bruxelles: Meline, Cans, 1860), p. 107; cf. *Nostromo*, 1904, pp. 379–82. Conrad also consulted *The Autobiography of Giuseppe Garibaldi*, tr. Alice Werner, 1889: see Hans van Marle: 'Conrad and Garibaldi', *The Ugo Mursia Memorial Lectures*, ed. M. Curreli (Milano: Mursia, 1988), pp. 337–52.
26. *CWW*, pp. 156–7.
27. *Nostromo* (1904), p. 286; *CWW*, p. 154.
28. *Nostromo*, p. 424; cf. pp. 423, 425.
29. *Wild Scenes in South America*, republished as *Travels and Adventures in South America* (London: Sampson Low, 1868), p. 164.
30. *Nostromo*, p. 355. (I preserve the erroneous 'Signora'.)
31. Páez: *Travels and Adventures*, p. 169; *Nostromo*, p. 348.
32. Eastwick: *Venezuela* (London: Chapman & Hall, 1868), p. 195; *Nostromo*, p. 323.
33. *Nostromo*, p. 392; *Venezuela*, p. 196.
34. *Venezuela*, p. 75; *Nostromo*, p. 102.
35. *Venezuela*, p. 76.
36. *Venezuela*, pp. 144–5.
37. *Venezuela*, p. 26.
38. *Nostromo*, p. 57; Masterman: *Seven Eventful Years in Paraguay* (London: Sampson Low, 1869), p. 228.
39. 'Berón': *Nostromo*, pp. 312–14; 'Román': Masterman, p. 287; 'Maiz' (correctly 'Maíz'): *T.P.s' Weekly*, IV, pp. 165–6; Masterman, p. 277.
40. Masterman, p. 54 (the incorrect grave accents are Masterman's); *Nostromo*, p. 87.
41. Masterman, pp. 18–19; *Nostromo*, pp. 197–8.
42. Burton: *Letters from the Battle-Fields of Paraguay* (London: Tinsley, 1870), p. 39.
43. 'Decoud': p. 285; 'Gould': pp. 126, 166, 328–30; 'Rincón': pp. 107, 261.
44. *Bouvard et Pécuchet* (Paris: Garnier, 1954), p. 266.

114

45. These critics and scholars include Paul Kirschner, Yves Hervouet and Owen Knowles. My discussion is particularly indebted to: Kirschner's *Conrad: The Psychologist as Artist* (Edinburgh: Oliver & Boyd, 1968); Hervouet's 'Conrad and Anatole France' (*Ariel*, I, 1970, pp. 84–99); Knowles's 'Conrad, Anatole France, and the Early French Romantic Tradition: Some Influences' (*Conradiana*, XI, 1979, pp. 41–61); Hervouet's 'Conrad's Relationship with Anatole France' (*Conradiana*, XII, 1980, pp. 195–226); and Hervouet's 'Conrad and Maupassant: An Investigation into Conrad's Creative Process' (*Conradiana*, XIV, 1982, pp. 83–111).
46. See Joseph Conrad: *The Nigger of the 'Narcissus'*, ed. Cedric Watts (London: Penguin Books, 1988); and Cedric Watts: *Joseph Conrad: A Literary Life* (London: Macmillan, 1989), pp. 42–4.
47. *Nostromo*, pp. 423, 425. France: 'Mérimée' [1888] in *Œuvres complètes*, VI (Paris: Calmann-Lévy, 1926), p. 383. (My translation.)
48. France: *Œuvres complètes*, VI, p. 377. *Nostromo*, p. 187.
49. Flaubert: *L'Éducation sentimentale*, I (Paris: Société des Belles Lettres, 1958), p. 88. (My translation.) *Nostromo*, p. 129.
50. Hervouet: 'Conrad and Maupassant', *Conradiana*, XIV (1982), pp. 100–102.
51. *Nostromo*, p. 457. France: *Balthasar*, in *Œuvres complètes*, IV (Paris: Calmann-Lévy, 1925), p. 127.
52. *Nostromo*, p. 22. *L'Éducation sentimentale*, I, p. 93. (My translation.)
53. *Nostromo*, pp. 54, 422–3. *L'Anneau d'améthyste*, in *Œuvres complètes*, XII (Paris: Calmann-Lévy, 1927), p. 6.
54. *Nostromo*, p. 326. *L'Anneau d'améthyste*, p. 221.
55. *Nostromo*, p. 442. France: *Le Lys rouge*, in *Œuvres complètes*, IX (Paris: Calmann-Lévy, 1927), p. 144.
56. 'Author's Note' to *Nostromo* (London: Dent, 1918), p ix. France: *Les Opinions de M. Jérôme Coignard*, in *Œuvres complètes*, VIII (Paris: Calmann-Lévy, 1926) p. 455.
57. *LCG*, p. 128.
58. *LCG*, p. 84.
59. *LCG*, p. 149.
60. *Speaker*, 24 February 1900, p. 564.
61. *Tennyson's Poetry*, ed. R. W. Hill (New York: Norton, 1971), pp. 147–8.
62. *The Wealth of Nations* (Harmondsworth: Penguin Books, 1982), p. 512.
63. ibid., pp. 507–8.
64. *Macaulay's History of England*, I (London: Dent, 1906), pp. 209, 320–21.
65. 'Chartism': *Critical and Miscellaneous Essays*, V (London: Chapman & Hall, 1869), p. 378; 'Corn-Law Rhymes': *Critical and Miscellaneous Essays*, IV (London: Chapman & Hall, 1888), p. 205.
66. *LCG*, pp. 71, 65.
67. *LCG*, pp. 56–7.
68. *White Nights and Other Stories*, tr. C. Garnett (London: Heinemann, 1918), p. 62.

69. *Hamlet and Don Quixote*, tr. R. Nichols (London: Henderson, 1930), p. 11.
70. *Nostromo*, pp. 443, 167, 319, 412.
71. *Nostromo*, p. 423; *Notes on Life and Letters* (London: Dent, 1949), pp. 34, 109.
72. *Nostromo*, p. 367; *Victory* (London; Dent, 1948), pp. 91–2.
73. *The Foundations of Empirical Knowledge* (London: Macmillan, 1958), p. 78.
74. Friedrich Nietzsche: *Werke in Drei Banden*, III (München: Hanser, 1960), p. 314: '*die Wahrheiten sind Illusionen, von denen man vergessen hat, dass sie welche sind*'. Arthur Schopenhauer: *Essays and Aphorisms*, tr. R. J. Hollingdale (Harmondsworth: Penguin Books, 1970), p. 68.
75. *LCG*, p. 65.
76. Marlow: '*Heart of Darkness' and Other Tales*, ed. C. Watts (Oxford: Oxford University Press, 1990), p. 172. Calderón: *LL*, II, p. 286; JB, pp. 190, 448–9, 492–3. Decoud: *Nostromo*, p. 209.
77. *A Common Sky* (London: Sussex University Press, 1974), pp. 146, 262.
78. *LCG*, p. 65.
79. '*Heart of Darkness' and Other Tales*. p. 172. *Lord Jim*, ed. C. Watts and R. Hampson (Harmondsworth: Penguin Books, 1986), p. 274.
80. *CLJC*, II, p. 418.
81. *Nostromo*, p. 32.

PART 4 (pp. 52–92)

1. *Return to Yesterday* [1932] (New York: Liveright, 1972), p. 33. See also Ford's letter to George Keating, quoted in F. R. Karl: *Joseph Conrad: The Three Lives* (New York: Farrar, Straus & Giroux, 1979), p. 558.
2. *CLJC*, III, pp. 120, 142, 167.
3. The commentators include Mizener, Najder and Karl. See *JCC*, pp. 299–300; F. R. Karl: *Joseph Conrad: The Three Lives*, p. 558.
4. See *Nostromo*, ed. K. Carabine (Oxford: Oxford University Press, 1984), p. 583.
5. Arnold Kettle: *An Introduction to the English Novel*, vol. II (London: Hutchinson, 1967), p. 67.
6. p. 63.
7. George M. Barringer: 'Joseph Conrad and *Nostromo*: Two New Letters', *Thoth*, X (Spring 1969), pp. 20–24. Quotation from p. 24.
8. pp. 357, 103.
9. *Oxford Companion to English Literature* (Oxford: Oxford University Press, 1985), pp. 704–5.
10. George M. Barringer: op. cit., p. 24.
11. *Classical Literary Criticism*, ed. T. S. Dorsch (Harmondsworth: Penguin Books, 1965), pp. 43–4.
12. *The Common People* (London: Fontana, 1984), p. 119.
13. 'I felt.....I wasn't getting the point,' said Naipaul. '*Nostromo* [was] a

confusion of characters and themes, which I couldn't get through at all.' *The Return of Eva Perón* (London: Deutsch, 1980), pp. 211, 213.

14. Wilhelm Liebknecht: *Briefwechsel mit Karl Marx und Friedrich Engels*, ed. G. Eckert (Mouton: The Hague, 1963), p. 304. (Original in German.)

15. *Manifesto of the Communist Party* (Moscow: Foreign Languages Publishing House, 1957), p. 78.

16. p. 70.

17. pp. 434, 443.

18. *Manifesto*, p. 51.

19. 'Author's Note' (1920) to *Under Western Eyes* (London: Dent, 1947), p. x.

20. *The Semiotics of Poetry* (Bloomington and London: Indiana University Press, 1978), p. 12.

21. *Shelley's Defence of Poetry*, ed. H. F. B. Brett-Smith (Oxford: Blackwell, 1972), p. 56; *Russian Formalist Criticism: Four Essays*, ed. L. T. Lemon and M. J. Reis (Lincoln, Neb.: University of Nebraska Press, 1965), p. 12.

22. See Ian Watt: 'Pink Toads and Yellow Curs', *Joseph Conrad Colloquy in Poland*, ed. R. Jabłkowska (Wrocław: Ossolineum, 1975), pp. 11–31.

23. Gérard Genette: 'Discours du récit', *Figures III* (Paris: Éditions du Seuil, 1972), pp. 78–80.

24. J. W. Beach: *The Twentieth Century Novel: Studies in Technique* (New York: Appleton-Century-Crofts, 1932), pp. 364–5.

25. Ian Watt: *Joseph Conrad: Nostromo* (Cambridge: Cambridge University Press, 1988), p. 37.

26. p. 21. Later editions changed 'peripeties' to 'passages'.

27. Blaise Pascal: *Pensées*, tr. A. J. Krailsheimer (Harmondsworth: Penguin Books, 1966), p. 95. Cf. Arthur Schopenhauer: *The World as Will and Idea*, I, tr. R. Haldane and J. Kemp (London: Routledge & Kegan Paul, 1961), pp. 266–7.

28. p. 379.

29. p. 480. Later editions change 'successes' and 'greater' to 'triumphs' and 'greatest'.

30. p. 380.

31. *Modern Poetry and the Tradition* (Chapel Hill: University of North Carolina Press, 1939), p. 167.

32. Hernández: p. 303. Carlos IV: p. 40.

33. JB, p. 301.

34. *Conrad the Novelist* (Cambridge, Mass.: Harvard University Press, 1958), pp. 215, 206.

35. pp. 422–3, 425.

36. p. 413.

37. LCG, p. 65.

38. *Notes on Life and Letters* (London: Dent, 1949), p. 109.

39. p. 442.

40. pp. 423, 32.

41. p. 455.
42. *Scritti Conradiani* (Milano: Mursia, 1983), p. 210.
43. p. 64.
44. *Notes on Life and Letters*, p. 107.
45. Guerard: *Conrad the Novelist*, p. 177.

PART 5 (pp. 93–105)

1. Holograph inscription in T. J. Wise's copy of *Nostromo* (in the British Library: Ashley 463).
2. Theodore G. Ehrsam: *A Bibliography of Joseph Conrad* (Metuchen, NJ: Scarecrow Press, 1969), p. 289.
3. *British Weekly*, 10 Nov. 1904, p. 129; *Daily Telegraph*, 9 Nov. 1904, p. 4; *Manchester Guardian*, 2 Nov. 1904, p. 5.
4. *LCG*, p. 158.
5. *Speaker*, NS XI (12 Nov. 1904), pp. 138–9.
6. *Conrad: The Critical Heritage*, ed. Norman Sherry (London: Routledge & Kegan Paul, 1973), p. 161.
7. *LCG*, p. 157.
8. p. 266.
9. pp. 425, 426.
10. p. 159.
11. *Conrad the Novelist*, pp. 199–202.
12. *LL*, II, p. 296.
13. *Spectator*, 24 April 1936, p. 758.
14. *The Great Tradition* (Harmondsworth: Penguin Books, 1962), pp. 248, 17, 211, 215–16, 218–19.
15. Kettle: *An Introduction to the English Novel*, vol. II (London: Hutchinson, 1967), p. 66.
16. Kettle, p. 69.
17. Kettle, p. 72.
18. Eagleton: *Criticism and Ideology: A Study in Marxist Literary Theory* (London: Verso, 1978), pp. 137, 138, 140.
19. *CLJC*, II, pp. 348–9.
20. *Criticism and Ideology*, p. 7.
21. Jameson: *The Political Unconscious: Narrative as a Socially Symbolic Act* (London: Methuen, 1981), p. 270.
22. *Nostromo*, p. 197.
23. Said: 'Through Gringo Eyes', *Harper's Magazine*, 276 (April 1988), pp. 70, 71.
24. *Nostromo*, p. 145.
25. pp. 140, 330.
26. p. 194.
27. Said, p. 71; *Nostromo*, p. 155; but I quote Conrad's probable source, Páez's *Travels and Adventures*, pp. 473–4.

28. *Nostromo*, p. 139.
29. p. 191.
30. Said, p. 72.
31. *Nostromo*, p. 85.
32. Said, p. 70.

PART 6 (pp. 106-11)

1. 'The Eighteenth Brumaire of Louis Bonaparte', in Marx and Engels: *Selected Works*, I (Moscow: Foreign Languages Publishing House, 1958), p. 247.
2. *Nostromo*, p. 8.
3. p. 377.
4. p. 42.
5. p. 21.
6. p. 18.

7.2 Bibliography

TEXTS

At the time of writing, there exists no authoritative scholarly edition of *Nostromo*, though such an edition has been commissioned by Cambridge University Press. Useful paperback texts include the Penguin version, edited and introduced by Martin Seymour-Smith (1983), and the World's Classics version, edited and introduced by Keith Carabine (1984). The latter provides informative extracts from the serial in *T. P.'s Weekly*.

LETTERS

Material concerning the genesis of *Nostromo*, and particularly the role of R. B. Cunninghame Graham, can be found in *Joseph Conrad's Letters to R. B. Cunninghame Graham*, edited by Cedric Watts (London: Cambridge University Press, 1969). With briefer paraphernalia, this correspondence is being reprinted in the volumes of *The Collected Letters of Joseph Conrad*, edited by Frederick R. Karl and Laurence Davies (Cambridge: Cambridge University Press, 1983 onwards).

BIOGRAPHICAL STUDIES

Biographies which give ample attention to *Nostromo* include the following. Jocelyn Baines: *Joseph Conrad: A Critical Biography* (London: Weidenfeld & Nicolson, 1960); Frederick R. Karl: *Joseph Conrad: The Three Lives* (New York: Farrar, Straus & Giroux, 1979); and Zdzisław Najder: *Joseph Conrad: A Chronicle* (Cambridge: Cambridge University Press, 1983).

Critical Studies: Nostromo

CRITICAL AND SCHOLARLY STUDIES

F. R. Leavis: *The Great Tradition* (London: Chatto & Windus, 1948; Harmondsworth: Penguin Books, 1962); Robert Penn Warren: 'Introduction' to *Nostromo* (New York: Random House, 1951); Arnold Kettle: *An Introduction to the English Novel*, vol. II (London: Hutchinson, 1953); Albert Guerard: *Conrad the Novelist* (Cambridge, Mass.: Harvard University Press, 1958); Eloise Knapp Hay: *The Political Novels of Joseph Conrad* (Chicago and London: Chicago University Press, 1963); Avrom Fleishman: *Conrad's Politics* (Baltimore: Johns Hopkins, 1967); Paul Kirschner: *Conrad: The Psychologist as Artist* (Edinburgh: Oliver & Boyd, 1968); Juliet McLauchlan: *Conrad: Nostromo* (London: Arnold, 1969); Norman Sherry: *Conrad's Western World* (London: Cambridge University Press, 1971); *Conrad: The Critical Heritage*, edited by Norman Sherry (London and Boston: Routledge & Kegan Paul, 1973); Terry Eagleton: *Criticism and Ideology* (London: Verso, 1978); J. A. Verleun: *The Stone Horse* (Groningen: Bouma's Boekhuis, 1978); Fredric Jameson: *The Political Unconscious: Narrative as a Socially Symbolic Act* (London: Methuen, 1981); Ian Watt: *Joseph Conrad: 'Nostromo'* (Cambridge: Cambridge University Press, 1988); Edward Said: 'Through Gringo Eyes' (*Harper's Magazine*, April 1988).

The magazines *Conradiana* (Lubbock, Texas: Texas Tech University) and *The Conradian* (London: Joseph Conrad Society) have featured a variety of essays on *Nostromo*.